BCL - 3rd ed.

Approaches to
American Economic
History

APPROACHES TO
AMERICAN ECONOMIC
HISTORY

Edited by

George Rogers Taylor

and

Lucius F. Ellsworth

Published for the
Eleutherian Mills-Hagley Foundation

The University Press of Virginia
Charlottesville

0942113

82314

The University Press of Virginia

Copyright © 1971 by
the Eleutherian Mills–Hagley Foundation

First published 1971

ISBN: cloth, 0-8139-0343-2; paper, 0-8139-0375-0
Library of Congress Catalog Card Number: 74-158808
Printed in the United States of America

Contents

0942113

82314

Introduction

A SEMINAR for college students majoring in history held in the autumn of 1968 and sponsored jointly by the history department of the University of Delaware and the Eleutherian Mills–Hagley Foundation provided the occasion for the lectures printed in slightly revised form in this volume. The seminar leaders, chosen because of their interest in the respective fields, were asked to regard their task as primarily pedagogical. They were to introduce students to a field of study, not to prepare papers for the benefit of their colleagues or other specialists. The success of the participants in achieving this objective encouraged this publication, which it is hoped will provide a useful manual for history students whether or not their primary interest lies in a study of economic history.

No fixed guidelines or structural uniformities were imposed on the contributors as complete freedom of style and procedure seemed desirable. Each lecturer indicates at least implicitly that he is dealing with *an* approach, not *the* approach, to economic history. Nevertheless, the perceptive reader may find it interesting to attempt to discover the extent to which each author, perhaps unconsciously and despite his own intention, makes a favorable case for the usefulness or importance of the approach which is the subject of his remarks.

The lectures are entitled "approaches" rather than "essays on methods" because their aim is not to introduce the students to techniques or methods as such. It was assumed that the members of the seminar had at least some acquaintance, for example, with statistical, economic and sociological theory. The study of history requires diverse approaches, and for each of these there is not a single appropriate method but suitable methods which need to be discovered and explored. As he confronts historical problems the student's skill will be tested by his ability to combine and modify the available approaches. As Hugh G. J. Aitken suggests in the first essay in this volume, the student, if sufficiently imaginative, may even develop his own approach.

The first five essays present approaches which do not use or at least do not stress quantification. In general they follow familiar paths, but each presents a synthesis which is innovative in some respects. Thus Aitken's essay on entrepreneurship provides a fresh view of an important influence on economic history by one who has made important contributions to this approach. Alfred D. Chandler, Jr.'s lecture on narrative history gives renewed emphasis to the growth of the business system as an institution. The stages approach dealt with in the third essay is as old as recorded history; yet the recent tour de force in this area by W. W. Rostow has given new life to analysis by stages and caused it to be discussed around the world. The economic interpretation of history, whether Marxian, Beardian or of some other variety, though often buried never fails of vigorous rebirth. Its treatment by Stephen Salsbury should prove provocative for students and produce critical fire from both the extreme right and left. Perhaps the least quantitative of all the approaches is Thomas C. Cochran's. His sociological-psychological emphasis is interestingly new and experimental.

Of the three quantitative essays included, that on the input-output system by Dorothy S. Brady is the newest and least developed for historical purposes. Heretofore used primarily for forecasting economic trends or describing contemporary flows, this system's promise for future historical studies warrants careful exploration. Robert E. Gallman's and Lance E. Davis's lectures well supplement each other. Gallman provides the student with a detailed analysis of a still unsolved problem in the measurement of American economic growth. Davis, on the other hand, deals comprehensively with the scope and method of the "new" economic history, illustrating the strengths and weaknesses of the quantitative-analytical-theoretical approach which characterizes it.

The approaches selected for consideration in this lecture series are obviously not the only useful or desirable ones. Other paths to historical understanding such as the geographical, demographic or technological might have been selected.

The approach which the economic historian finds most congenial and with which he feels most competent often determines his choice of the problem to which he applies himself. Thus training in archeology may attract the economic historian to the study of artifacts which throw light on the changing economic organization of some primitive people. Special interest in international trade theory may tempt him to investigate the operation of the gold standard as it functioned for a few decades in the late nineteenth and early twentieth centuries. Or training in statistical methods may encourage a student investigator to observe changes in national income over a period of years. This matching of the special interest of the scholar with the nature of the problem to be investigated is on the whole natural and desirable, though enthusiasm for a favored approach may lead to overemphasis or to exclusive dependence upon it. A Marxian class-conflict interpretation which may throw much light on the nineteenth-century struggles in Western Europe will, at least in the view of most scholars, contribute little to an understanding of the westward movement in the United States. Likewise a technological or stages emphasis may prove of limited use in exploring the retarded development of the industrial system in the southern United States.

Although a student decides to investigate a particular problem because the indicated approach suits his special interest, competence or temperament, the complexity of the historical process soon reveals unexpected facets. Scratching the surface of one problem uncovers further problems; discovering an answer to one question brings three other unanswered ones into the open.

As a result, when the economic historian deals with a subject of appreciable magnitude, he discovers the inadequacy of a single-track approach and finds a variety of methods and approaches indispensable. For example, suppose a student well trained in the use of statistics raises the question of how rapidly New York City grew during some relatively short period, say 1840 to 1860. Though the data are by no means perfect or complete, he can unearth much in regard to the changing numbers, age distribution, sex, national origin and occupation of the rapidly growing population. This is only a beginning. Many other statistics are available for the measurement of growth or change. The investigator collects and tabulates such series as those on foreign and domestic trade, shipbuilding, residential construction, banking and prices. When all these figures are assembled, reduced to indexes, and perhaps extended by the use of proxies, they call for interpretation. When it is asked why New York City grew more rapidly than its rivals, the statistical series have to be evaluated, and explanations involving judgments not possible on the basis of numbers alone must be attempted.

Related aspects of the problem can seldom be ignored. Able business leaders migrating to New York City from New England contributed to the vigorous growth of that port. Why did the northeastern states have a surplus of such talent? Why did young men migrate to New York? And why were they unusually successful in this urban milieu? Answers to these questions necessarily require sociological and psychological analysis. Nor is it sufficient merely to bring in the reports from these specialists, for a truly satisfactory answer cannot be found merely by adding up the various approaches and dividing by x. The weights to be assigned to each of the findings cannot be arrived at by a formula. No approach or combination of approaches gives a simple answer to a complex problem. And no model includes universally acceptable assumptions for large problems.

The student of economic history will do well to bear in mind that, no matter what approach or approaches he may find useful, he operates in part, at least, outside the field of the natural sciences—that the paradigm of physical explanation cannot always be carried over into history and the social sciences. The deductive model is seldom suitable for explaining social actions. The adding up of events does not answer the question of *why*, if for no other reason than that analysis in the social sciences is relative to the culture and values existing at a particular time and place.

In a very real sense the historian deals constantly, and cannot avoid dealing, in limited generalizations. He obviously does so when he uses such words as *democracy* or *industry*. Pure constructs like Max Weber's "ideal types" may be useful for those who seek wide generalization. But overarching theories of society must be looked upon with skepticism. Based as they typically are on the metaphor of growth taken over from nature or the construct of necessity derived from the physical sciences, they are, whether reported by the ancient Greeks, Karl Marx or Arnold Toynbee, will-o'-the-wisps. Man depends on metaphors for understanding and communication, but so simple and attractive a metaphor as youth, maturity and decay is not a proof.

Human history of whatever variety can be understood only in terms of actors having aims, purposes and values. In the physical sciences testability and deductibility are the prime methods of explanation. In the social sciences the search is for intelligibility or understanding, an effort which involves explication qualitatively different from that in the physical sciences. Man understands or comprehends the behavior of other men only by means of the symbols and metaphors common to a given society.

To some extent the economic historian becomes involved, it is true, with the materials and methods of both the physical and the social sciences. The history of technology includes the ways in which changes in machines and the use of power have affected the organization of production and distribution and the level of living. But the propensity to invent or to innovate and the readiness or unreadiness of a particular culture to exploit particular inventions depends on many factors, not the least of which are the interests, enthusiasms and values of the people concerned, their culture and their institutions. The law of diminishing returns as usually stated in its most general form is a physical law, and as such it may well have relevance to economic situations whether past or present. But as soon as this law is stated in terms of alternative costs or human choices, as it must be in meaningful human history, the student of economic history must be on his guard, for the generalizations now made will involve assumptions about human behavior. For example, how are costs defined? Costs to whom? Is labor considered solely as a factor of production or also as a unit of consumption?

Designed, as this book is, for the student planning further explorations in history, it is appropriate that in addition to arming him with a variety of useful approaches it should post a few warning signs to alert him to the land mines and ambuscades which may endanger his progress.

The economic historian may on occasion develop a model, a paradigm or an ideal type to assist him in understanding a historical problem. As explicit models are at present much in favor it is especially important for him to learn to recognize at least a few of their most common seductions and limitations. Some writers insist that all assumptions must be clearly recognized and explicitly stated. But the difficulties of following such counsel are commonly very great, often insuperable. Such concepts as a perfect vacuum or perfect price elasticity at a point may be conceptualized and prove significant in solving physical or mathematical problems. But how different, for example, is the assumption which the economic historian makes concerning the propensity to save. This propensity or tendency may be measured, if the data are available, for some particular time and place and also for the same place after a time interval. But the usefulness of all this may be minimal. If, for example, the propensity to save is merely the amount saved over a time period, we have no more than tautology. We have no explanation of why the propensity exists, why it changes or remains constant, or how important any change may be.

Another danger is that the model itself may become prescriptive; instead of serving as a neutral tool it may influence the selection of materials and determine the course of the investigation. Thus it may be, for example, that Douglass C. North in his model of pre-Civil War economic development in the United States was led unconsciously to accept as fact the major dependence of the cotton South upon grain from the Ohio and Upper Mississippi valleys—a "fact" concerning which writers were not in complete agreement and upon which recent research has cast increasing doubt. North doubtless made an honest choice on the basis of the materials available, but he may have done so after a less critical examination than he would have made if the information had not fitted so comfortably into his pattern.[1]

No one knows better the dangers of the quantitative approach than those who apply statistics to the solution of concrete historical problems. As Gallman and Davis point out in their essays, the student who makes use of a numbers approach will have to be ever watchful. This is especially true when, as is usually the case, he is dealing with numerical data which have been subjected to adjustment or manipulation. Even such apparently straightforward figures as those constituting price series are not as chastely innocent as they seem. Changes in units of measure present problems, as do variations in grade and quality. Gaps occurring in the original data may have to be filled in by interpolation or extrapolation, possibly by using series from distant markets as proxies. When price or production figures are combined in indexes, difficult decisions must often be made as to the base period to be chosen, the weights to be assigned to different series and the proper procedure to be followed when new items replace old ones in the index. All these considerations, as well as others, may vitally affect the meaning and significance of the index.

In recent years *growth* has become the magic word. All the ap-

[1]Douglass North, *The Economic Growth of the United States, 1790–1860* (Englewood Cliffs, N.J., 1961).

proaches discussed in this volume are basically designed to explicate economic growth. The usefulness of this emphasis is not questioned, but it is a tricky term which probably should be printed in bright red ink, signaling caution. Although seldom noted, *growth* almost always refers to *measured growth*; that is, it includes only those aspects of development which can be quantified. Not only do problems arise as to what is being included and what left out, but the process of measurement involves complex calculations, among which the index number diffiulties noted above are only a part.

Growth is most often expressed as production or income per capita and then explicitly, or more often implicitly, used as a measure of welfare. Frequently no account is taken of the distribution of the measured income among different classes or groups. Even more important, consideration is seldom given to the simultaneous production of illth or diseconomies, external as well as internal. The output or productivitiy of a paper mill, for example, may be measured by the volume or value of the paper manufactured. But such a mill adds to the total measured productivity of a community not only by the amount of the incomes earned by the mill workers but by the income received by the doctors who must attend those workers and members of the community who are made ill by the polluted air and by the wages of the house painters, window washers and laundry employees who "benefit" from the employment provided by the effects of smoke and gas. The measured growth of the community also increases if the mill contaminates the water supply sufficiently to force expenditures for reservoirs and aqueducts to bring pure water from distant sources.

One other example must suffice. In the small cities common in the United States in the ante-bellum years, craftsmen and mechanics often labored twelve or more hours a day, working within their own homes or within easy walking distance of them. Today city workers seldom toil more than seven or eight hours a day, but they no longer can eat their lunches at home, and many have to spend from one to three hours each day coming and going to work. Nevertheless, in terms of measured growth the community advantage is very great, for the workman must now ride to work, causing the product per capita of the community to grow tremendously because of the value of the automobiles, buses and railroad cars which must be built, the wages of those who operate and service them and the value of the coal and gasoline consumed. Growth is indeed wonderful, but the student may well be on his guard when using a concept which so abounds in obscurities and paradoxes.

The lectures which constitute this volume can do little more, of course, than alert the student to the possibilities, the advantages and disadvantages, of various approaches to economic history. For the student who wishes to pursue his studies further, the Bibliography, prepared by Lucius F. Ellsworth, provides additional references on each essay as well as on business history. Especially recommended are the readings in the second section of each list, for they provide actual specimens of the approach discussed in each lecture.

GEORGE ROGERS TAYLOR

Approaches to
American Economic
History

I The Entrepreneurial Approach to Economic History

Hugh G. J. Aitken

IN FAIRNESS to the reader I should make clear my own position with respect to the entrepreneurial approach to economic history. I have done little research or writing in this area for the past ten years, and I have no plans to do any in the immediate future. I write, therefore, not as an active practitioner of the approach, but rather as one who has certain qualifications for reporting on it. These qualifications stem from my long and close association with several of the scholars who pioneered in developing this approach and from the fact that I was at one time fortunate enough to be a member of the Research Center in Entrepreneurial History at Harvard University.

It can hardly be disputed that in general the best man to describe a particular approach or technique is one who is currently using it. There is, however, something to be said on the other side. Active practitioners of an approach tend to feel their commitment to it as a personal matter, not a coldly intellectual one. They are in a sense in love with it, and it is hard for them not to wax lyrical when describing its virtues. This is particularly true if, as so often happens, approaches are regarded as competitive rather than complementary. We should, therefore, remind ourselves regularly that theories and approaches are tools, not ends in themselves. Which you choose to use depends on the problem you hope to solve and the data you have available or can find. When you choose one approach rather than another, you should do so on strictly pragmatic grounds, not because one advocate speaks with greater eloquence.

For students of economic history, and particularly for those of the younger generation, the real challenge is, in any event, not that of mastering existing approaches, but that of developing new ones. Any list of approaches is a list of things that have already been tried. None of them should satisfy the next generation of economic historians. If any one of them does, the outlook for the future of our discipline is not a happy one.

The entrepreneurial approach to economic history has never been a thoroughly systematized, closely articulated body of theory. It has meant different things to different people. It has reflected their varying assumptions regarding what counts in economic history and their varying views regarding what are economically relevant problems. For this reason it makes little sense to talk about the entrepreneurial approach without talking about the men who have used it and the work they have done.

Let me begin, then, by introducing the names of three scholars, each of whom made his distinctive contribution to the entrepreneurial approach: Jean Baptiste Say, Joseph A. Schumpeter and Arthur Harrison Cole.

To Say we must give credit for the clearest and most succinct statement of the classical view of entrepreneurship.[1] Briefly stated, the entrepreneur is for Say that man who buys the factors of production at a certain price, combines them and sells their output at an uncertain price. Three points deserve comment here. Note first Say's emphasis on the human element. The factors of production do not combine themselves. They require human intervention, and this intervention is a contribution to production distinct from but no less important than the contribution of the conventional factors of production.

Second, even at this early date there is an emphasis on uncertainty and risk-bearing. The entrepreneur buys at certain prices and sells at uncertain ones. In fact, this bridging between certainty and uncertainty is part of his characteristic function. Say's entrepreneurs live in a world of uncertainty and differ in the skill and/or luck with which they cope with uncertainty. In Say's view this is both the source of and the justification for entrepreneurial profits.

Third, the entrepreneur, as Say sees him, chooses the production function. Say does not emphasize innovation, or the introduction of new production functions, but he does stress the element of deliberate choice. Which production function to use is not a cut and dried matter; it involves judgment; and it introduces the possibility of error.[1]

[1]Compare Joseph A. Schumpeter, *History of Economic Analysis* (New York, 1954), 555, and Thomas C. Cochran, "Entrepreneurship," *International Encyclopaedia of the Social Sciences* (New York, 1968), 5, 87–91.

Jean Baptiste Say, in short, conceived of the entrepreneur as a decision-maker, an organizer and a coordinator. Equally important is the fact that, in his view, the economic process in the real world required such an agent; and further, that a good model of the economic process had to include entrepreneurship as one of its elements. These two statements are not quite the same thing. The English classical economists who were more or less contemporary with Say did not introduce into their theories an entrepreneur in the sense of a separate, identifiable agent in the production process.[2] The people that Say might have labeled entrepreneurs would be thought of, in the classical English model, as a particular type of labor input. And in this model the process by which prices and quantities are brought into equilibrium, given the relevant demand and supply schedules, does not logically require the introduction of the concept of entrepreneurship.[3] The same is true today. Pick up any standard introductory textbook of economics and you will find the theory of price and output determination under perfect competition elegantly presented without any reference to the entrepreneur at all. In such a model the concept of the entrepreneur is not logically required (although that of a profit-maximizing firm is), and it is quite proper to eliminate it. This does not mean that the people who write these textbooks fail to appreciate the fact that, in the real world, decisions on prices and quantities are taken by real people, any more than Adam Smith or David Ricardo can be charged with failing to realize it.

If I appear to dwell unnecessarily on this simple point, the reason is that it has led to frequent and quite unnecessary misunderstanding. There is really no point in castigating economic theorists because they have left the entrepreneur out. And there is equally little point in sneering at historians for choosing to study an economic function

[2]The prominent exception is John Stuart Mill.

[3]William J. Baumol has expressed the point precisely: "The model is essentially an instrument of optimality analysis of well-defined problems, and it is precisely such (very real and important) problems which need no entrepreneur for their solution" ("Entrepreneurship in Economic Theory," *American Economic Review*, LVIII [May 1968], 67). Harvey Leibenstein points out, however, the two critical assumptions upon which the conventional theory rests: that the complete set of inputs is specified and known to all actual or potential firms in the industry, and that there is a fixed relation between inputs and outputs ("Entrepreneurship and Development," *ibid.*, 73).

which, in certain particular theoretical models, is not separately identified. You can build models (of price determination, let us say, or of economic development) which do require the concept of entrepreneurship, and you can build models which do not. Some economic historians find it interesting to work with models that give entrepreneurship a pivotal role, but this surely does not mean that a truth has been disclosed to them that is hidden from others.

Say is a remote figure in the history of economic thought, and for some younger economists the same can probably be said of Joseph Schumpeter. But not for me, because Schumpeter was still teaching at Harvard when I went there as a graduate student in 1948 and in fact was one of the senior members of the Harvard Research Center in Entrepreneurial History. Few of us at that time realized how fortunate we were to be able to study under a man like Schumpeter. There was a tendency even then to regard his theory of economic development, of which the Schumpeterian entrepreneur was an essential part, as rather dated and simplistic. (I have, incidentally, been intrigued recently to find that many of my own students now react very favorably to Schumpeter's theory of capitalist economic development, particularly as presented in his *Capitalism, Socialism, and Democracy.* Clearly there is something in Schumpeter's vision highly congenial to the New Left.)

Schumpeter's entrepreneur differs from Say's in one important respect. His function is not that of combining the factors of production in known, familiar ways, as was true with Say. It is that of introducing the new and unfamiliar. The entrepreneurial function, in a word, is essentially linked with innovation. The entrepreneur who does not innovate is, in the Schumpeterian system, a contradiction in terms. The agent whom Say designated as the entrepreneur is, for Schumpeter, the manager.

This change of definition, I hardly need to stress, is fundamental and reflects the very different purposes for which the two men needed the concept of entrepreneurship. Say thought he needed it to explain the determination of prices and outputs in a system of static equilibrium. The entrepreneur selects among known production functions in such a way as to produce any specified output at minimum average costs. Then he selects his most profitable output by the criterion of profit maximization. Schumpeter needed the concept of entrepreneurship to explain economic development: not the determination of prices and outputs in static equilibrium but the introduction of new production functions, new goods, new sources of supply, new markets and so on. Entrepreneurship is the act of innovation, the creative response by which firms, industries and whole economies break out of the circular flow of the known and the familiar and move on to new potentials.

But, having said this, one must immediately add that Schumpeter and Say have, in their view of the entrepreneur, one important feature in common. Both deny that economic processes are automatic. In Say the combination of the factors of production, even in known ways, does not proceed without human intervention; and in this human intervention, because of the unavoidable presence of uncertainty in any process that involves present investment for future returns, there is the possibility of success and failure, of economically correct and economically incorrect choices. Schumpeter is even more explicit. To him the essence of entrepreneurship is the creative response, correctly defined as the doing of something that could not be predicted, even with full knowledge of the entire preceding conjuncture. This is how novelty enters, how development (as distinct from mere growth) takes place.

It is true that Schumpeter, when speaking for the record, was careful to stipulate that innovations could be humble as well as impressive—the frankfurter sausage as well as the nuclear power plant— and that entrepreneurs did not form a single social class or represent a single personality type. There was always present, however, in Schumpeter's concept of the entrepreneur something of the heroic, something larger than life-size. His entrepreneur was a creative leader, not quite as other men are. And there was something about creativity and leadership which Schumpeter preferred not to analyze, perhaps because he thought it could not be analyzed. *Ignorabimus*, it has been said, is not a proper slogan for a scholar; but it might well have been Schumpeter's answer if pressed hard to list the ingredients of creative entrepreneurship. This is why there has always been an element of the mystical about the Schumpeterian entrepreneur, an element alien to the positivistic thinking that pervades the social sciences today. It is clear, in any event, that Schumpeter's vision of the entrepreneur is not Say's. Say's entrepreneur one may visualize as the owner of the corner grocery store, Schumpeter's as the great captain of industry. The entrepreneurial approach will mean one thing to you if you think in Say's terms, but quite another if you follow Schumpeter.

Arthur Harrison Cole, unlike the other two scholars in my trio, is not yet a figure of history. On the contrary, he is very much alive and active today. He is included in my list for the good and sufficient reason that the entrepreneurial approach to economic history was his creation. Say, Schumpeter and others used the concept of the entrepreneur in their theories; Schumpeter even made entrepreneurship the essence of his model of capitalist development. But Cole was the first to conceive of entrepreneurial history as a field of study; and it was under his leadership and inspiration that the first explorations of this field were carried out. And so it is important that I convey to you some idea of what Cole was trying to do, and why he thought it needed to be done.

Let me try to place you in the world of American economic historians in the middle and late forties of this century. The first thing to bear in mind is that it was a relatively small world. The Economic History Association was founded only in 1940, and during the war years it did not grow very much. Its annual meetings were still friendly affairs where everyone knew everyone else. There were not many new recruits to the field each year, and not many jobs to be filled either. Intellectually, economic history was still very much under the influence of Edwin F. Gay, who during his years at Harvard had done much to establish it as a recognized and respectable discipline. Two of Gay's former students, N. S. B. Gras and Arthur H. Cole, both at Harvard Business School, were among the more prominent figures in the field.

Economic history in the United States at that time had two problems. One was its slow rate of growth and the difficulty it was experiencing in recruiting talent in the graduate schools. The other was a tendency toward internal division by the formation of subfields like agricultural history, industrial history, labor history and, of course, business history. The Economic History Association and its journal had been founded largely to counter this fissiparous tendency, but the attempt had not been wholly successful. In particular, business history, under the leadership of N. S. B. Gras, lived a life of its own.

There was marked specialization of personnel—with a few notable exceptions like Thomas C. Cochran and Shepard B. Clough, business historians wrote business history and economic historians did not—and there was little exchange of ideas. One reason for this state of affairs was that, at the time, business history had few ideas to offer and was in the market for even fewer.

The situation clearly called for entrepreneurship, both the managerial coordinating variety of Say and a dose of Schumpeterian creative leadership. This was supplied by Arthur Cole, working with his colleagues on the Committee on Research in Economic History, itself financed and in part created by the Rockefeller Foundation. In 1944 the Committee sponsored a document defining the areas in economic history that, in its judgment, deserved intensive cultivation in the years ahead. Two of these were termed major fields: the role of government in the economy and the history of entrepreneurship. Two were minor fields: the history of banking and the history of the corporation.

This manifesto of 1944, if I may so term it, served as a guide for the operation of the Committee on Research for the next ten years, and it would require no prolonged research to demonstrate its impact on what American economic historians chose to do over that period. Goals had been clarified, priorities stated and a sense of direction acquired by a discipline badly in need of it. But in addition, in the prolonged debates and committee meetings that preceded the appearance of the document, a good deal of preparatory thinking had taken place concerning, for instance, how one might go about studying such matters as the history of entrepreneurship. Some of this preparatory thinking is reflected in Cole's presidential address to the Economic History Association in 1946, a deservedly famous paper with the title, "An Approach to the Study of Entrepreneurship."

Cole's conception of the entrepreneur might be interpreted as a synthesis of Say and Schumpeter, except that from the beginning he insisted on regarding entrepreneurship as a social process. Who "the entrepreneur" in a firm might be interested him less than what entrepreneurship was and how it functioned. It was, he said, an "integrated sequence of actions, taken by individuals or by groups operating for individual business units, in a world characterized by a large measure of uncertainty"; in basic functions it boiled down to "innovation upon a solid operational base achieved through the medium of business decisions." And, in a phrase later to be often quoted, he claimed forthrightly that to study the entrepreneur was to study "the central figure in modern economic history and . . . the central figure in economics."

Over the next twenty years Cole's ideas were to undergo considerable extension and elaboration, but he never really departed far from this view. And it was essentially around this conception that entrepreneurial history developed, particularly at Harvard where Cole, Schumpeter, Cochran, Leland Jenks and others formed the Research Center in Entrepreneurial History. The publications and working papers of this group are readily available and do not need to be reviewed here. Let me instead comment upon one aspect of the matter that has, I think, been insufficiently emphasized up to now.

One of Cole's objectives, explicitly stated in this first major paper, was to bridge the gap that had appeared between business history and economic history. This was the point of that crucial phrase in his definition: "actions taken by individuals or by groups *operating for individual business units*" (my italics). Indeed, he was trying to do more than join business and economic history. The concept of entrepreneurship, as he saw it, could become one of the major integrative ideas of the social sciences. "It may be contended," he argued, "that a study of entrepreneurship in its historical setting provides an opportunity to synthesize the work going forward in economics and in business administration, in economic history, business history, and social history, in the history of entrepreneurial thought and the history of social thought." This was the point of the whole endeavor: not to carve out yet another esoteric specialty, but to integrate and synthesize, to develop an area of study and a point of view that specialists in many fields would find interesting and useful.

It has always been my personal belief that the possibility of reestablishing fruitful liaison with business history was, for Cole, a prime objective. Business history was the other half of the Gay tradition, and Gay himself would never have thought of it as an independent discipline, shut off from the mainstream of historical studies. What better way to bring about a reunion than by elaborating the implications of entrepreneurship? It is time, I think, to call attention to the fact that, in pursuing this particular objective, Cole achieved striking success. There is, to be sure, some sterile and dull business history still being written and published. It surely differs little in this respect from other kinds of historiography. But the best work in the field today is very different from what business history was when Gras's influence was at its height. In parceling out credit for this happy outcome I would not wish to shortchange the business historians themselves, whose open-mindedness and willingness to change has been matched only by their urbane perseverance in the face of continuous slights and snubs from the rest of the historical profession. But I think some of the laurels are due to Cole as well. The entrepreneurial approach survives as a vital and creative force today partly because the business historians have nourished it.

It cannot be said that equal success marked the attempt to make entrepreneurship serve as an integrative concept in other areas. Some useful work was done in the application of formal sociological theory to historical materials, and a great deal was done to clear up confused thinking about entrepreneurship itself. By the time the Center had been in existence for a few years, most people associated with it had given up the kindergarten game of "Find the Entrepreneur," had stopped agonizing over whether X was or had ever been an entrepreneur and were coming to think of entrepreneurship either as a social role or as an economic function. The emphasis, in other words, shifted away from thinking of entrepreneurship as an individual, personal thing and toward conceiving of it as a characteristic of organized systems of behavior, formal or informal—systems which included business firms and other kinds of social units as well. Research became directed toward exploring the conditions conducive to this kind of behavior, including both what we might call the environmental conditions and those subsumed under the concept of personality. All this was very helpful and intersting to the participants and materially assisted in the production of a series of monographs, the Studies in Entrepreneurial History, which were well received at the time and are still respected today. But the impact of the Center's work on fields of inquiry other than business history was slight.

Particularly was this true of economics. I do not believe that the twenty years or so of organized and subsidized work on entrepreneurship had any impact at all on the development of economic theory. Sometimes, indeed, I think nothing has much impact on the develop-

ment of economic theory except the unfolding logic of the subject itself and perhaps (although Professor George J. Stigler would differ
with me on this) policy problems of acute current concern.[4] But there
were obvious reasons why entrepreneurship had particular difficulty
in this respect. The concept was intrinsically difficult, perhaps impossible, to quantify. In fact, it was not easy even to make it operational, that is, to define it in such a way that you could say precisely
what observable phenomena were included and what were not. But
beyond this there is the fact that the economic theorists felt no need
for the concept: the models they were building worked pretty well
without it; the policy problems with which they concerned themselves
did not seem to require it, although in connection with the underdeveloped areas there was an uneasy suspicion that one had to face up
to entrepreneurship somehow or other. The big, important development in economics in the late 1950s was the revolution in instruction
that made econometrics part of the standard tool kit of every young
economist, a revolution which has had a decided impact on historical
studies in the form of the "new" economic history. This was, if you
will pardon me, where the action was. The people working on entrepreneurship were trying to introduce into economics a concept which,
as far as the Anglo-American tradition was concerned, had never
been regarded as really necessary (*pace* Frank Knight). They were
swimming against the tide; economics was moving in quite a different
direction.

Perhaps this was unfortunate. It is all very well to say that no one
can quantify entrepreneurship; but no one has ever made clear to
me what kind of unit one dollar's worth of capital is either, and we
have recently become rather uncomfortable about reducing labor
to a single elementary unit. Where would classical economics have
been without the concept of utility? Part of the reason why the work
on entrepreneurship made little impression on economics was simply
that, if one took it seriously, its implications for the inherited corpus
of Anglo-American economic theory (a body of thought essentially
mechanistic in character) were rather subversive. Much better,
surely, to ignore it and hope that it would go away. In some subfields of economics this was not difficult. The work of people like

---

[4]Stigler, "Economic Theory and Economic Policy," in *Essays in the History of Economics* (Chicago, 1965), 16–30, esp. 20–21.

Edith T. Penrose and William J. Baumol, for example, had a much greater impact on the theory of the firm than did the work of the entrepreneurial historians.[5] But economists like Bert F. Hoselitz, Albert O. Hirschman and Harvey Leibenstein, working on economic development problems, found it harder to ignore the entrepreneurial element, and in the newly popular field of productivity analysis, considerations of entrepreneurship were never far below the surface.

Economic historians in this country and elsewhere generally found entrepreneurial history a congenial and interesting approach. I am not aware of anyone active in the profession in the 1950s who took a stand in opposition to the new approach, although to some it did smack a trifle of revisionism, a subtle means of rebuilding the shattered reputations of the robber barons and so on. It was the appearance of the new economic history, with its emphasis on econometric testing of hypotheses, that cast the entrepreneurial approach into the shade and made it appear somewhat old-fashioned. This was completely understandable. Scholarship has its fashions just as women's clothing has, and the New Look of one decade must give way to the miniskirt of the next. It was surely inevitable, or so at least it seems in retrospect, that the advent of econometrics into the standard graduate school curriculum in economics should have repercussions on economic history.[6]

It is not my purpose here to discuss the new economic history, and I shall resist the temptation to do so. I might repeat my earlier warning, however, that the choice of an approach to use in economic history depends in large measure on the problem you wish to solve and

[5]Penrose, *The Theory of the Growth of the Firm* (New York, 1959); Baumol, *Business Behavior, Value and Growth* (New York, 1967). See also Richard M. Cyert and James G. March, *A Behavioral Theory of the Firm* (Englewood Cliffs, N. J., 1963).

[6]It may not be amiss to point out here that Robert W. Fogel ("The New Economic History I. Its Findings and Methods," *Economic History Review*, 2nd ser., XIX [Dec. 1966], 642) does less than full justice to his predecessors in dating the appearance of the new economic history by the two essays written by Alfred H. Conrad and John R. Meyer in 1957. The first published specimens of work clearly of this type are to be found in *Explorations in Entrepreneurial History*, the journal of the Harvard Center. It was in 1955 that *Explorations* published Meyer's article on the use of input-output techniques to assess the causes of British economic retardation in the late nineteenth century; Lance E. Davis's articles on sources of industrial finance in the textile industry appeared in the same journal in April 1957 and Michael C. Lovell's article on the Bank of England as lender of last resort in October 1957. There is more continuity in the discipline than we sometimes like to admit.

the data you intend to use. I have never found anything antithetical in
the entrepreneurial approach and the new economic history. But then
I don't consider it perverse to like both Scotch and bourbon. I could
wish that all exponents of the new methodology were equally catho-
lic in their tastes. Some of their comments on the entrepreneurial
approach (mostly uttered *sotto voce*) suggest difficulty in grasping
the fact that theories can move on different levels of abstraction.
There has been, for example, a tendency to argue that entrepreneurship is not important because, in some cases that have been examined,
the economically appropriate thing seems to have been done at the
right time. Thus, for example, a particular technological change
may turn out to have been introduced just when it became profitable
to do so. Or a particular transportation system may turn out to
have been built just when the rate of return on the capital invested
equaled the current interest rate on securities of similar risk. Much
of the work done in the new economic history seems to turn up results of this kind. They have suggested, in other words, that the market seems to have worked with reasonable efficiency as a device for
allocating resources, an idea always comforting to economists since
it reinforces their assumptions. I would be the last to question the interest and importance of findings of this kind; but I cannot understand how they can be interpreted as implying that entrepreneurship
is unimportant. On the contrary, do they not suggest that, in the cases
examined, entrepreneurship was highly effective? If, in a particular
restaurant, one finds that meals are always excellently cooked and
served on time, is one entitled to conclude that there are no cooks in
the kitchen? If a particular airline always manages to keep its flights
on schedule, does that suggest that it has dispensed with the services
of pilots and flight controllers?

What these examples do suggest is not that entrepreneurship is of
slight importance, but that its functioning can, in some fortunate
places and times but not in others, be taken for granted as not part of
the problem. This does not entitle the historian to dismiss it from
consideration any more than it entitles the engineer to forget about
gravity. The very presence of rapid development in a particular economic system is prima-facie evidence of effective entrepreneurship,
because it means that potentials for innovation are being promptly
exploited. Why people should think they are being scientific and hard-

headed when they talk about the market but regard it as a kind of mysticism to talk about entrepreneurship is frankly beyond my understanding.

But enough of these family squabbles. What did the entrepreneurial approach amount to in practice? What kind of questions were asked, and what kind of problems were posed? If you used the entrepreneurial approach, you found yourself studying business firms, businessmen, business institutions and business practices. At least, this was so if your interest was in the so-called free-enterprise or capitalistic economies, which have historically been characterized by considerable decentralization of economic decision-making. There is in principle no reason at all why you cannot study the state or any of its creatures as entrepreneurs, but in fact little has been done with that idea.

You studied these businessmen and business firms not as individual isolated entities but as components of business systems. This sounds very impressive, but what exactly does it mean? Conventional business history in the N. S. B. Gras era took as its primary concern the individual business firm and focused its attention on the internal administration of that firm. Entrepreneurial history, in contrast, broadened its field of view to include the external relations of the business firm and the businessmen who composed it. Where did they come from? From what social strata were they recruited, and how? What kind of people were they? Where did they get their ideas, their conceptions of what they ought to do, of what was right and proper? What was the role of business in society, and who defined that role? What was expected of it, by whom? What influence did that social institution we call business have on politics, on aesthetics, on literature, on art? And what were the reciprocal influences? In what ways did business firms constitute a business system? How did the secularly increasing division of labor among business firms contribute to the extension of the size of the market? And how did this increase in scale contribute to the advance of productivity? Where did innovations come from, and how were they imitated and diffused throughout the economy?

Implicit in all these questions was a refusal to be bound by the conventions of business history as it existed at that time. These conventions assumed that the internal affairs of a business firm could be studied by themselves, without reference to the complex links that bound these affairs to society at large. Cole's insight—his "vision," in Schumpeter's terminology—was precisely this: that business is part of society and cannot be studied without full awareness of the two-way relationships between social values and business practices. The business firm, as Cole has continuously emphasized, is part of a system of interacting institutions which society tolerates and controls by virtue of the productivity that results. But there is no autonomous sanction for business. There never can be. As part of society, in an organic sense, business behavior both has an impact on and is influenced by the values of the social structure in which it functions.

From the professional economist's point of view, as distinct from that of the historian, entrepreneurial history is part of the attempt to explore the origins of changes in productivity. When seen in this light the entrepreneurial approach certainly need present no apology for its objectives, for the analysis of productivity has, since the 1940s, become an almost obsessive activity among economists. As a result of the empirical work of such men as Edward F. Denison, John W. Kendrick and Zvi Griliches and of the theoretical contributions of Robert M. Solow, Evsey Domar and a host of others, it is now widely understood that increases in output can be explained only in part by increases in the inputs used to produce that output.[7] How small this part is as compared with the residual that *cannot* be explained by increases in inputs is a matter of intense concern and dispute in the profession (though there is no truth to the rumor that the American Economic Association at one time considered offering a prize to the first economist who could reduce the residual to zero). A great deal depends on whether you think it makes sense to separate increases in inputs from increases in quality embodied in those inputs. But if you do think that this procedure makes sense, you are likely to

[7]Denison, *The Sources of Economic Growth in the United States and the Alternatives before Us*, Committee on Economic Development, Supplementary Paper No. 13 (New York, 1962); Kendrick, *Productivity Trends in the United States* (Princeton, N. J., 1961); Griliches, "The Sources of Measured Productivity Growth: United States Agriculture, 1940–60," *Journal of Political Economy*, LXXI (August 1962), 331–46; Solow, "Technical Change and the Aggregate Production Function," *Review of Economics and Statistics*, XXXIX (August 1957), 312–20; Domar, "On Total Productivity and All That," *Journal of Political Economy*, LXX (Dec. 1962), 597–608.

find that your data show that only a small fraction of the measured increases in output can be ascribed to increases in inputs. Most must be explained by increased output per unit of input. Somehow or other we seem to be able to bake larger and larger cakes without requiring proportionately larger and larger quantities of ingredients. This is what is meant by productivity increase.

How can this kind of thing happen? There are only two possible ways: either the quality of the inputs used is changing, or the inputs are being combined more effectively. These alternatives summarize the two principal approaches to productivity and analysis: first, through examination of technological change, the advance of knowledge, education, investment in human beings and other ways of bringing about qualitative change in inputs; and second, through examination of changes in production functions, or the recipes by which inputs are combined.

These are the two main avenues to an understanding of productivity change. They are also, and they always have been, the dominant concerns of entrepreneurial historians. From Say to Schumpeter to Cole, people who talked about entrepreneurship were talking about the combination of factors of production, the introduction of new combinations and (a matter particularly stressed by Cole) the improvement in the quality of this kind of action over time. And they were talking about this kind of thing because they knew, intuitively in some cases, for good theoretical reasons in others, that it is one of the fundamental economic processes that have made the modern world what it is.

I am not claiming that the scholars associated with the Harvard Research Center thought about their subject in these terms. And I am far from suggesting that the residual in productivity analysis can simply be equated with entrepreneurship. My point is rather that, using a vocabulary of their own, the entrepreneurial historians were feeling their way toward a problem of central importance to economic theory, economic history and economic policy. If this is the case, I cannot be overly concerned about the future of the entrepreneurial approach to economic history, for what was essential and relevant in that approach will undoubtedly survive and flourish. Words indeed are but "wise men's counters," and if it helps communication with our theoretical brethren to talk more about technological change and productivity growth and less about entrepreneurship, so be it. I may be pardoned, however, a slight skepticism on the point. Economic historians have a professional affection for concepts that are useful even if not precise—witness, for example, the amazing survival power of that oft-disproved notion, the Industrial Revolution. Unless the breed changes its semantic habits quite markedly, I expect that talk about entrepreneurs and entrepreneurship will be heard for many years to come.

II Business History as Institutional History

Alfred D. Chandler, Jr.

MY POINT of view in this essay is twofold. First institutional history must be more than mere narrative, although the narrative aspect always remains important. Second, it is only by treating business history as institutional history that this subdiscipline can make a substantial contribution to economic and general history.

One reason business history can make a special contribution to economic history is that the present mathematical orientation of theoretical economics has turned economic historians, trained as economists, away from institutional analysis. The new economic history has genuine value for business history, as well as broader economic history. Lance Davis, Robert Gallman and others will undoubtedly point this out in their essays in this volume. Certainly the work of such scholars as Douglass C. North and Albert Fishlow has added greatly to the understanding of the American economic past. Their interest, however, is with that which is quantifiable. The emphasis on and manipulation of numbers, so central to the new economic history, provides natural limits to its descriptive and analytical use.

The increasing specialization exemplified by the mathematical approach has enhanced the opportunities of historians who use nonquantifiable data and who are asking questions that cannot be answered by numbers alone. There is a real need for trained historians to continue to use that discipline's traditional sources—letters, memoranda, periodicals and general accounts. Scholars not particularly interested or adept in mathematics can become better economic historians, not by trying to master the new economics, but by using more fully the heritage of institutional history. In many areas, this heritage can provide tools for analyzing economic change as effectively as and in greater depth than has yet been done by the compilation and manipulation of numbers.

As institutionalists, business historians can contribute not only more usefully to economic history but also to the understanding of general American history. In fact, they have done so already. John Higham, in an incisive analysis of the writing of American history, points to two major recent trends. One he terms psychological history, the other institutional. He first describes the "psychologizing trends": "In recent years scholarly journals have teemed with articles and university presses with books on historical myths, symbols, images, and the like. A psychological approach may, if it continues to gain momentum, reopen every question in American history." In reviewing what he considers the long-term significance of the approach, Higham says:

Fortunately, American historians have not yielded wholly to the psychologizing trend. Among those who still respect the force of overt principles, a strain of rationalism persists. It is also reappearing among a small but rising number of historians who are taking a fresh look at organizational patterns. The latter wish to know how groups and agencies—such as political parties, corporations, and communities—have molded behavior and regulated the distribution of power. Deriving partly from studies in entrepreneurial and business history and partly from contemporary American sociology, this kind of history is less concerned with motives than with structure and process. It shows men managing and being managed through rational systems of control and communication. Perhaps we may call this the new institutionalism; for it is bringing back to life a morphological study of organizations, now freed from the formalistic, evolutionary emphasis of nineteenth century scholarship.

Although institutionalists thus far have not gone much beyond the monographic level, the breadth and importance of their contribution seem sure to grow.[1]

This able and eminent American historian, who is in no sense a business or economic historian, is suggesting the opportunities available to the heirs of N. S. B. Gras and Arthur Cole. It seems significant that Higham here and elsewhere in his book says nothing of the other subdisciplines of nonquantitative economic history such as agricultural, labor or even technological history.

Higham's emphasis on the contributions of business and entrepreneurial historians suggests their special opportunities. In the

---

[1] Higham, Leonard Kriger and Felix Gilbert, *History: The Development of Historical Studies in the United States* (Englewood Cliffs, N. J., 1965), 230–31; ©1965 by the Trustees of Princeton University, quoted by permission of the publisher, Prentice-Hall, Inc.

United States (and in Western Europe and Japan) businessmen have been at the center of economic change. Moreover, in the United States and much of the West, economic changes in the past century have helped to transform the basic ways of life and, therefore, the polity and the society as well as the economy.

Businessmen and institutions have played a large role in some of the fundamental changes in American life since 1800. During the past century and a half, Americans have experienced a transformation of the economy from one that was agrarian and rural to one that is urban, industrial and technologically sophisticated. This change has affected every aspect of American life. One result has been the rise of large-scale organizations, which have become even more pervasive in the economic sphere than in political and social life. Another is the revolution in modern technology and science, which has had a more direct impact on more people through changing consumer goods and modes of communication and transportation than through military, space or other governmental programs. Such changes have played a critical part in the depersonalizing and dehumanizing of society. They have also contributed to the rise of the so-called meritocracy and other aspects of the modern world.

In all these changes, businessmen had more influence than farmers, laborers, technologists, scientists or even politicians and government officials. Whether this influence has been desirable or not, it remains that the businessmen planned, financed and managed the railroads and the older textile, coal and iron and agricultural processing trades, as well as the newer oil, chemical, electrical machinery, machine tool, automobile and aircraft industries. It was the businessmen who financed and managed the factories, organized the cartels and associations and created the giant corporations that characterize so much of our economy today. Businessmen set up research and development departments, hired the technologists and made decisions about the production and sale of laboratory products. Even today, despite the growth in the power and activities of the government, labor unions and farm organizations, businessmen continue to dominate the production and distribution of American goods and services and the short- and long-term allocation of the nation's economic resources.

Since the businessmen have been so central to change in America,

their historians are in a strategic position to analyze and explain
major aspects of the nation's history. Much still must be done if we
are to understand business and change in the American economy.
These opportunities will be still greater if institutional history is
defined as more than just the study of organizations. This style of
history should include the study of regularized patterns of action between organizations, and between organizations and individuals, for
such patterns are essential to the continuing operation of any complex economic system. They integrate that system with the political
and social systems and the larger national culture. We understand
far too little about any of these fundamental relationships. For
example, suprisingly little is known about the process of distributing
goods from the producer to the ultimate consumer in nineteenth-
century America.

Business historians, however, cannot take real advantage of their
subject until they become better historians by making the fullest use
of existing generalizations, concepts and models and by developing
new ones for their own use. Here is precisely the value of considering
business history as part of institutional history. There is a rich heritage of knowledge, data and methods concerning institutions and institutional change. This knowledge has been developed for more
than a century by historians, economists and sociologists.

The greatest pioneer was in fact an economic historian who became a founder of modern sociology, Max Weber. Weber not only
provided an enormous amount of data on comparative and changing
institutions, but he developed that most useful and now most pervasive of analytical tools, the model. The following is his definition of
the intellectual construct which he called "an ideal type" and which
can be considered as a verbal or nonmathematical model.

An ideal type is formed by the one-sided *accentuation* of one or more points
of view and by the synthesis of a great many diffuse, discrete, more or less
present and occasionally absent *concrete individual* phenomena, which are
arranged according to those one-sidedly emphasized viewpoints into a unified *analytical* construct. In its conceptual purity, this mental construct cannot be found empirically anywhere in reality. It is a *utopia*. . . .

It has the significance of a purely ideal *limiting* concept with which the
real situation or action is *compared* and surveyed for the explication of certain of its significant components. Such concepts are constructs in terms of
which we formulate relationships by the application of the category of ob-

jective possibility. By means of this category, the adequacy of our imagination, oriented and disciplined by reality, is *judged*.[2]

One of Weber's most useful ideal types for the business historian was his model of bureaucracy. Some attributes of this construct will be found in all large-scale organizations, but none have them all. By comparing the model to a specific organization, the historian has an excellent way of launching his analysis of nearly any large modern economic unit. Weber's other concepts, such as class and status, are as valuable.

Max Weber is also important because he had a significant influence on the economists and sociologists of the next generation, though less so on historians, particularly American historians. His two most important interpreters were Joseph Schumpeter and Talcott Parsons, both of whom taught at Harvard.

Schumpeter was Weber's most noteworthy successor as an economic sociologist and historian. He developed Weber's ideal types and became more interested in explicit models with a mathematical orientation. Although much more of a mathematically oriented economist than Weber, Schumpeter was concerned with institutional arrangements. He was interested in the changing role and activities of the entrepreneur, the family firm, the large bureaucratic corporation, the structure of industry and the larger cultural environment. Schumpeter was unfortunate in the timing of the publication of his major work, *Business Cycles*. It was overshadowed by the publication of John Maynard Keynes's *General Theory* three yeare before, for Keynes turned economists to macroeconomics and mathematics and away from institutional analysis. Even microeconomics became highly mathematical and noninstitutional.

Fortunately, Weber's tradition was carried forward by his foremost American pupil, the sociologist Talcott Parsons. Parsons and his students have defined and explored the relationships of individual personality to institutions, institutions to larger systems (political and social as well as economic) and all three (personality, institutions and systems) to the still broader areas of cultural attitudes and values. His definitions and distinctions are of great value in understanding

[2]Quoted in H. Stuart Hughes, *Consciousness and Society* (New York: Alfred A. Knopf, Inc., 1958, © 1958 by H. Stuart Hughes), 312–13.

changing business and economic activities and institutions. For example, in analyzing relationships between men, institutions and systems, he suggested the importance of differentiating between affectivity and affective neutral attitudes and values; between particularistic and universalistic norms; between quality and performance (i.e., ascribed and achieved status); and between collective orientation and self-orientation. According to Parsons, such culturally defined differences become routinized into normative patterns of action. Often, however, changes in technology or population create new functional demands on existing institutions and so alter patterns of behavior and in time even change the culturally defined values.

Besides Parsons, Schumpeter and Weber, institutional historians have other intellectual reserves to tap. There are the students of organization theory whose basic ideas are derived from Frederick W. Taylor, as well as Max Weber. And there are the small group theorists who come from psychology and who learned much from Elton Mayo and Fritz Roethlisberger and the experiments they conducted in industrial plants. Historians can learn a great deal from the writings of Chester Barhard, Herbert A. Simon, James G. March, George C. Homans, Robert F. Bales and other practitioners of these two approaches to group action.

I have briefly reviewed the work of these notables to illustrate that if business history is considered a part of institutional history, it becomes heir to a major intellectual heritage and tradition. Such a heritage can provide an invaluable intellectual base. Surely, one weakness today in the writing of American history is the failure of both students and their teachers to appreciate such heritages.

Although the business historian can draw upon this fund of ideas, I also want to stress the fact that he must develop his own concepts and verbal models. A historian's task is not merely to borrow other people's theories or even to test their theories for them. It is to use existing concepts and models to explore the data he has collected in order to answer his own particular questions and concerns. If a concept does not seem to help, he should throw it away. If it seems to have value only if it is modified, then he should modify it. And always he should work at developing his own analysis.

Let me suggest an example of how this heritage of institutional history can be used to help understand and explain changing patterns of business and economic activities. By focusing on the process of production and distribution within an industry, a sector of the economy, or possibly even the economy as a whole at one period of history, one might develop a static and then a dynamic model. One could begin by considering two aspects of the process of production and distribution: first, the coordination of the flow from the initial producer to the ultimate consumer and within each unit along the line of flow; and, second, the procedures of costing carried out during that flow both within and between the units. Then one would examine how coordination and costing affected the structure of the firms and the structure of the industries involved. Next, one might ask how these factors helped to determine the nature of decision-making and the types of decision-makers concerned. What, for instance, was the influence of procedures of coordination and costing on the recruitment, training and career patterns of decision-makers? Finally, it would be necessary to convert this static model into a dynamic one by considering the impact of technological and market changes on the ways of coordination and costing and, therefore, on structure, decision-making and decision-makers. Having set up a model along these lines, we could go into the data for one time period, for instance from 1850 to 1880 or 1900 to 1920, to see how reality as reflected in the data available is similar to or different from the model. Although this method will not bring the precise results an economist might like, it should be of value in learning how and why the economy worked and how and why it changed. Here one is tempted to recall the words of one mature critic of modern social sciences who said it was better to be right in a general way than wrong in a precise one.

In conclusion, let me make a few summary points. First, I do not think that business history is or needs to be as detailed, disparate, diffuse or even as dull as it may often appear. Second, if American business history is seen as a part of institutional history, it has a genuine opportunity to contribute to economic and general American history and to make full use of a major intellectual heritage. Third, the business historian has an advantage over other institutional historians because his subjects have been the prime movers in an epoch in which economic change stimulated some of the most profound transformations in the ways of mankind. Fourth, and finally, he can use this advantage to make a major contribution to economic and general history only if he comes to know and makes full use of his existing intellectual heritage, and only if he does so in a way imaginative enough to generate his own concepts, models and other tools for the purpose of analyzing and explaining the changing patterns of business and economic action.

III Stage Theories of Economic History

George Rogers Taylor

STAGES, periods, eras and epochs are devices commonly adopted by historians, especially economic historians. They are the boxes, the pigeonholes, into which the elusive, tangled and intractable materials of history are filed in order to render them more manageable and comprehensible. The shapes, mutual relationships and capacity of these boxes provide the substance of this essay. Even the labels on these containers provide some interest. Consider, for example, the happy inspiration which led Walt W. Rostow to term his central stage of growth the "take-off." How much less attention his doctrine might have received if, following the preference of Simon Kuznets, he had chosen the jejune though descriptive title, "early modern growth stage." But the names chosen are probably not very significant. The Chinese, it will be remembered, called their disastrous attempt to accelerate economic growth the "Great Leap Forward."

The mere periodization of history may seem far removed from the concept of stages of development. But the similarities are substantial, the differences largely a matter of degree. Both concepts have to do with the selection of time periods convenient for the study of the past. For both the period chosen depends upon the questions raised, and each confronts the inescapable problem of explaining the transition from one period or stage to the next. Most general historians, when using such terms as periods or eras, ignore the need to explain the change from one epoch to another. The stages historian often centers attention on the transition, not infrequently stressing the discontinuities or revolutionary aspects involved in the succession of changes. He also may carry over into his explanation the pattern of unilinear or biological growth and so run the danger of confusing a metaphor with a law of development, simple succession with casual continuity.

That a book entitled *The Stages of Economic Growth* should, early in the 1960s, become the most widely read treatise on economic history, not only in the West but around the world; that it should be translated into well over a score of languages; that returning travelers should report it as popular reading by students and government administrators in the newest African states, in remote provincial cities of South America and in the capitals of Far Eastern nations; and that a group of leading economic historians of the Western world should travel to Konstanz, Germany, in 1962 for the purpose of discussing this study—all suggest that a stage approach to economic history merits serious consideration. No extended historical review of the development of stage theories is provided here, as useful surveys are available to the interested student.[1] Instead, after a brief review of some of the past attempts to formulate stage theories, attention will be centered on the stages of growth as developed in Rostow's writings, primarily on that part of his model having to do with the take-off.

If growth or change takes the form of sequential development over time, whether unilinear, circular or spiral, the successive steps may be designated stages. Such stages may be little more than convenient chronological divisions to assist in a largely descriptive treatment. But the concern here is with those schemes which develop the steps along with a more or less elaborately constructed system of relationships.

Only the briefest note will be taken of a few of the ambitious attempts to develop overarching theories encompassing the whole history of civilization. An early exponent of such a general theory was G. B. Vico, 1725, who adumbrated a circular law of development involving three phases: (1) the age of the gods (theocracy), (2) the age of heroes (aristocracy) and (3) the age of men (democracy). In time each stage developed excesses which led to its decay and emergence into the following stage. More familiar recent attempts at comprehensive theories are such imaginative constructs as those of Oswald Spengler and Arnold Toynbee.

Somewhat less sweeping in their theories were the writers belonging to the school of German historical economists. Their interests

[1]See Bert F. Hoselitz, "Theories of Stages of Economic Growth" in Hoselitz (ed.), *Theories of Economic Growth* (Glencoe, Ill., 1960), 193–238; and N. S. B. Gras, "Stages in Economic History," *Journal of Economic and Business History*, II (May 1930), 395–418.

usually represented a combination of political and economic factors. Thus Gustav Friedrich Schmoller saw development as taking place in five phases: village, town, territorial, national and finally world economy. His contemporary, Karl Bücher, proposed a shorter list of three stages: household economy, town economy and national economy. Although economic factors are basic in the system developed by Karl Marx, he also took note of political aspects in his well-known sequence of stages: primitive communism, feudalism, capitalism and socialism. His linear progression led ultimately to utopia, thus conforming to Judeo-Christian teaching. Finally it may be noted that N. S. B. Gras, writing in the third decade of this century, emphasized urban growth and, combining political and economic considerations, erected a system incorporating the following stages: collectional, cultural, nomadic, settled village, town and metropolitan.

Economic aspects of development can never be completely separated from other influences, but many of the attempts at erecting stage theories focus on economic phenomena. Such economic stages have been usefully defined by Gras as "socially competitive conditions in which a new method or institution rivals, then threatens, and finally outdistances an old one."[2]

The most usual formulation of economic stages before the Industrial Revolution appears to be one going back to the Greeks which was adopted by Adam Smith. It includes three steps: (1) hunting and fishing (savagery), (2) pastoral (nomadism) and (3) settled agriculture. Wilhelm Roscher of the German school of historical economists developed a more elaborate system which also emphasized agriculture. His stages were: hoe culture, burning and wild field-grass husbandry, the two- and three-field systems, field-grass husbandry, rotation of crops and garden culture. Much impressed by the economic development of England, Friedrich List, writing at the middle of the nineteenth century, went beyond these primarily agricultural stages and, accepting substantially Smith's first three stages, added a fourth, agricultural-manufacturing, and a fifth, agricultural-manufacturing-commercial. Frederick Jackson Turner's frontier thesis, which has greatly influenced American historical writing, is essentially a stage interpretation. He wrote: "As succes-

---

[2]"Stages in Economic History," 397.

sive terminal moraines result from successive glaciations, so each frontier leaves its traces behind it." So in his view the United States developed in successive waves or frontiers: that of the Indian, of the fur trader and hunter, of the cattle-raiser or miner, of the pioneer farmer, and finally that of the city dweller and manufacturer.

With the continuation of the Industrial Revolution, the growing output of industry and the maturing of capitalism, the interest of the builders of stages shifted away from agriculture. Thus at the beginning of this century Bücher developed a stage system consisting of housework, wagework (hardly a self-explanatory or useful step as developed by him), handicraft, putting-out and factory work. Bruno Hildebrand, an early member of the German school of historical economists, advanced a simpler system, one emphasizing a different facet of the economy. He listed natural, money and credit economy as the significant steps, a scheme which in the hands of his followers became more elaborate, though hardly more useful.

Another emphasis was that of Gras, who found the following states suitable for his purposes: prebusiness capitalism, petty capitalism, mercantile capitalism, financial capitalism and national capitalism. Much simpler was Joseph A. Schumpeter's two-stage system, which envisaged socialism replacing capitalism as monopolies arose and stagnation replaced innovation.

In recent decades economic historians have been especially interested in (1) the role of the entrepreneur and (2) measuring and accounting for economic growth. In respect to the former, Arthur H. Cole has suggested a three-stage approach in which the business leaders have been oriented successively toward community, industry and nation. As for economic growth, W. G. Hoffman, confining himself to an analysis of manufacturing development, has held that four stages can be "identified for all free economies." These progress from the earliest phase in which consumer-goods industries are of "overwhelming importance" to the fourth stage by which time "consumer-goods industries have been left far behind by the rapidly growing capital-goods industries." Another writer, Colin Clark, struck by the rapidly growing importance of service industries, has developed a threefold system in which the stages are respectively primary industry, manufacturing (secondary industry) and services (tertiary industry). Finally we come to Rostow, whose theory of stages has attracted such wide attention. It must be assumed that the reader is familiar at least with the broad outline of his thesis, which involves five stages: the traditional society, preconditions for take-off, take-off, drive to maturity and the age of high mass consumption.

The architects of stage theories or even those who merely divide history into convenient epochs may be under the impression that no normative element enters their thinking. They sometimes appear to believe that they are merely reasoning in conformance with reality. But the defense of such a position melts away under questioning. Obviously stages or periods are selected because of their significance in the view of their sponsors. They are significant because they help to answer important questions, that is, questions whose importance is recognized by the writer, not, it may be emphasized, because of the facts themselves. Facts, merely as facts, are quite without significance. Even if a theory of stages is admittedly a construct, a model which obviously departs from reality but is designed to be useful in analyzing and probing possible relationships, it must be remembered that the models chosen are those that appear to promise worthwhile insights. This is not reprehensible; it is merely unavoidable. It is of the essence of inquiry in the social sciences.

The periodization or stages system which a scholar develops is inevitably closely related to his interests. The representatives of the school of German historical economists who were so fertile in developing stage systems appear to have been thinking primarily in terms of the emergence of nation states, especially Germany and Italy. List stressed the need for tariff protection as he pleaded for the unification of Germany. Always he emphasized the "national interest." Even Karl Marx's most ardent followers would hardly deny that his unconcealed hatred for capitalism influenced the system of stages which he espoused. Rostow's equally tendentious argument dwells with obvious approval on the forces leading to the take-off and self-sustained economic growth. Surely no mere whim led him to entitle his major work, *A Non-Communist Manifesto.*

A subtly dangerous presupposition, buried more or less below the surface, impairs most stage theories. This arises from a tendency to regard the progression from one stage to the next as inevitable or irreversible, as somehow following the biological metaphor of growth as a natural and necessary development. Thus List believed in, and regarded as natural, progress toward a unified Germany. So also Marx not only described the class conflicts of presocialist stages but discerned in them the progress by which they would inevitably destroy the old societies and make way for communism. A similar belief in a necessary sequence of stages flourishes weedlike in the very center of Rostow's anticommunist garden.

Rostow does, it is true, recognize from time to time the danger of considering his progression of stages as preordained. He notes some variations from country to country and warns on the first page of his book that he "cannot emphasize too strongly at the outset, that the stages-of-growth are an arbitrary and limited way of looking at the sequence of modern history: and they are, in no absolute sense, a correct way."[3] And again he points out that he "does not pretend to explain all of history."[4] Nevertheless the sense of a pattern of forces working themselves out in a necessary series of stages throughout the world pervades the book. His stages of growth are presented, it will be remembered, as "an alternative to Karl Marx's theory of modern history." And he says explicitly, "These stages are not merely descriptive. They are not merely a way of generalizing certain factual observations about the sequence of development of modern societies. They have an inner logic and continuity. They have an analytic bone-structure, rooted in a dynamic theory of production."[5] Rostow is neither unintelligent nor dishonest but, as so often happens to system-builders, he becomes bemused by his own creation. He believes against his own better judgment, or at the very least gives the reader the impression he believes, that he has discovered laws of development or stages of growth whose progression is predetermined.

Most stage theories are enunciated as being applicable without limits of either time or space; List is a notable exception in that he explicitly excludes the tropics from his pattern of development. In the *Communist Manifesto* Marx appears to see the progression from primitive communism through class conflicts to utopia as the universal destiny. In this respect he is somewhat less explicit than Rostow, who presents his system as applying, with only minor variations, to

---

[3]Rostow, *The Stages of Economic Growth: A Non-Communist Manifesto* (Cambridge, Eng., 1960), 1.
    [4]*Ibid.*, 118.   [5]*Ibid.*, 12–13.

all countries which have been or are becoming industrialized, without respect to their economic maturity, their cultural history or their geographic location. This apparent acceptance of a universal pattern of growth independent of time and place has aroused substantial criticism. Alexander Gerschenkron has objected strongly to Rostow's position in this respect, insisting that the relative backwardness of a country serves as a crucial factor in affecting the path of its movement toward increased productivity. Thus he emphasizes the pressure on undeveloped nations resulting from the forwardness of others. He points to the influence which may be exerted by the availability of outside capital as well as improved techniques, which can often be borrowed even more easily than capital.[6]

The attempt to divide history into stages or periods tends to emphasize the discontinuities of historical development—at times it serves to overemphasize them. To some extent Rostow's take-off as well as Gerschenkron's "great spurt" seem to put too much stress on the transition, on a sharp break with the past which is by no means self-evident when one examines the course of development in such countries as Great Britain, France and the United States. But this is, in part at least, a matter of perspective. Taking the broad view, the changes of the last two or three centuries seem no less than revolutionary. Seen over any one or two decades the continuities often appear as the most impressive part of the picture.

Many of the older treatments merely describe or identify the stages, giving little heed to analyzing the mechanism of transition from one stage to the succeeding one. A chief merit of Rostow's study lies in the careful attention he gives to this crucial consideration. Passing over Rostow's interesting account of the transition from his first stage, the traditional society, to his second stage, the preconditions for take-off, we may note briefly some of the major and necessary developments in the preconditioning period which he stresses. Agriculture, he notes, must be improved so as to feed an increasing population and must permit, along with other developments, an increase in savings which will in turn encourage new investments. These will result in the creation of a minimum social

---

[6]Gerschenkron, "The Early Phases of Industrialization in Russia: Afterthoughts and Counterthoughts," in W. W. Rostow (ed.), *The Economics of Take-Off into Sustained Growth* (New York, 1965), 164–69.

overhead involving especially improvements in transport. Also new
leaders must arise in the pre-take-off period, a new elite which represents the values of a growing industrial society, rather than those
of the traditional landowning aristocracy. Competitive nationalism
and the demonstration effect of the most rapidly growing economies
also play an important role.

At the point of take-off a new tempo replaces the more measured
development of the preconditioning period. It may be triggered by
internal or external political developments, by revolution or war. At
any rate the prior development of the economy now promotes, in
Rostow's words, "a positive, sustained, and self-reinforcing response. . . . the result is not a once-over change in production functions or in the volume of investment, but a higher proportion of potential innovations accepted in a more or less regular flow, and a
higher rate of investment."[7] In the aggregate "the proportion of net
investment to national income (or net national product) rises from,
say 5% to over 10%, definitely outstripping the likely population
pressure . . . and yielding a distinct rise in real output *per capita*."[8]
Along with this emerge "one or more substantial manufacturing
sectors, with a high rate of growth."[9]

In the light of the emphasis which Rostow places on the dramatic
and radical nature of the take-off, it is noteworthy that other students
do not find closer agreement with his timing. For fourteen leading
countries, Rostow locates the decade when the take-off occurs. Yet,
despite the supposedly drastic or revolutionary nature of this phase
of development, most students of particular countries (England and
the United States are good examples) find the changes spread out
over a longer period than Rostow's two decades, and typically
they question his timing. In one of his later statements Rostow, while
asserting that the take-off "is a recognizable discontinuity in the
stream of history," admits there may be some question of locating
the "preceding decade" and that there is likely to be some expansion
of production in the industrial output in the pre-take-off decade.[10]
This last statement warrants scrutiny, for how recognizable is a
"recognizable discontinuity" preceded by "some" expansion of
production when "some" remains unspecified? Simon Kuznet's com-

---

[7]Rostow, *Stages of Growth*, 37.   [8]*Ibid.*   [9]*Ibid.*, 39.
[10]*Economics of Take-Off*, xx.

plaint concerning the fuzziness of the line between the preconditions and the take-off seems amply justified.

The critics of the Rostovian theory have often pointed out that the over-all pattern of savings, investment and growth in output per capita as presented in the Rostow pattern does not fit the actual course of events in most countries. The inductive studies do not yield results in conformity with Rostow's model. Saving and investment may actually prove to be as high in the pre-take-off period as in the following stage; the increase in savings may be primarily a resultant rather than a causal factor in the take-off. Per capita increases in production may depart appreciably from the predicted values. Simon Kuznets, for example, has examined the capital formation proportions during the take-off period for four countries which have been carefully studied: Great Britain, Germany, Sweden and Japan. In no case does he find a reasonably close conformance to the Rostow pattern. "I can only conclude," he says, "that the available evidence lends no support to Professor Rostow's suggestions."[11] Also A. K. Cairncross says,

There is undoubtedly some tendency for all the symptoms of rapid growth to show themselves simultaneously. But there is no invariable dependence of growth on a high rate of capital formation. . . . Moreover there is some justification for turning the causal relationship the other way around. If income is growing fast, investment opportunities are likely to be expanding even faster, so that the growth in income draws capital accumulation along behind it. The biggest influence on capital formation is market opportunity, and many types of capital accumulation are likely to be embarked on only when income is booming.[12]

In any case, studies of the factors responsible for recent economic growth in the United States cast serious doubt on the unique role claimed for increased investment. Thus, investigations by Edward F. Denison and Robert M. Solow attribute, at least for recent decades, from one-third to more than three-fourths of per capita growth in the United States to technological improvements and ascribe a relatively minor role to capital inputs.[13] Possibly recent

[11]Kuznets, "Notes on the Take-Off " in *ibid.*, 35.

[12]Cairncross, "Capital Formation in the Take-Off " in *ibid.*, 245.

[13]Denison, *The Sources of Economic Growth in the United States and the Alternatives before Us* (New York, 1962), and Solow, "Techanical Change and the Aggregate Production Function," *Review of Economics and Statistics*, XXXIX (August 1957), 312–20.

conditions are so different from those in the take-off period that this finding should not be taken too seriously. Nevertheless, it may well be emphasized that neither inductive studies nor recent attempts at analysis give support to the importance which Rostow ascribes to an increased supply of capital.

In defense of his analysis, Rostow has increasingly turned to disaggregation, emphasizing the role of individual leading sectors. Thus he identifies cotton textiles in Great Britain and railroads in the United States as energizing agents. One can quarrel with his specific analysis, as does Albert Fishlow whose studies downgrade the importance of railroads as a leading sector. Nevertheless, Rostow's emphasis on sectoral analysis and the spreading effects of such sectors, their linkages backward, laterally and forward, place a valuable emphasis on an area of inquiry which merits increased attention.[14] But even in developing this concept a tendency toward circular reasoning in Rostow's argument disturbs the careful reader. Thus in defining the take-off Rostow writes, "One or more modern industrial sectors take hold, with high rates of growth, bringing in not merely new production functions but backward and lateral spreading effects on a substantial scale."[15] The troublesome word here is "substantial." How substantial? Substantial enough to produce a take-off? Unfortunately this is the term we started out to define.

Once the take-off has been effected, according to Rostow, the process of growth proceeds automatically, or almost so, in an endless struggle against deceleration. This follows because, as the rate of growth of the leading sector gradually slows down, the stimulating effects on the economy of new sectors take over, providing the self-sustained growth which results from repetition of the take-off process with all its spreading effects. Although admitting that his process of self-sustained growth is not always completely automatic, Rostow says that any considerable turning back is unlikely, that in the long perspective the take-off is irreversible, like the loss of innocence, and growth becomes a powerful on-going process. Still, after approaching the very brink of this precipice of inevitability, he

---

[14]Much useful work has already been done. See, for example, Albert O. Hirschman, *The Strategy of Economic Development* (New Haven, 1966).

[15]Rostow, *Economics of Take-Off*, 8.

holds back, remarking prudently, "nevertheless, we still have much to learn about the longer spans of the industrialization process."[16]

What should be said in a general summary of the value of the stage approach, especially as developed by Rostow? On the debit side should be noted an oversimplification of the historical development, the incomplete and at times unconvincing explanation of the transition from one stage to another, and especially the tendency to ascribe a certain inevitability, naturalness and universality to the stage theory. The last is surely unfortunate in so far as it has confused a metaphor with a law of development and encouraged people in underdeveloped countries, those seeking to achieve a take-off, to put their faith in simple formulas for growth or to accept universal remedies for backwardness.

By his emphasis on leading sectors and on the linkages involved in growth Rostow makes an important contribution by raising old questions in new ways. But in this connection attention should be directed to Fishlow's perceptive review of *The Economics of Take-off*.[17] He contends that Rostow's sectoral analysis would have been strengthened had he given greater emphasis to the importance of leading sectors in promoting the diffusion of improvements in technology. The machines created to service one growing sector of industry almost always promote the development of methods and machine tools suitable for use in other areas, thus stimulating their rapid growth and possible emergence as leading sectors.

On the credit side, we should be grateful to Rostow for refocusing our attention on the Industrial Revolution and for his courageous attempt to study the pattern of modern industrial growth and to develop some meaningful generalizations concerning it. His willingness to generalize should stimulate others to try to improve on his pattern and should serve to remind those scholars who claim to stick to the facts that they also are generalizing covertly or unconsciously while Rostow does so openly. And, if the range of Rostow's theorizing seems too broad, we are reminded of the need of seeking at least limited generalizations and of exploring ways to make them more general and more meaningful.

The stages method of economic history has developed out of

[16]*Ibid.*, 11.
[17]Fishlow, "Empty Economic Stages," *Economic Journal*, LXXV (March 1965), 112–25.

descriptive and analytical categories which have long proved useful. Like all generalizations, stage theory inevitably involves simplification; it emphasizes uniformities and slights differences. Students will continue to use this approach, but they will require that the stage theories developed be suited to the ends sought. At the very least it must be recognized that by stating his thesis in challenging form Rostow has called attention to the possibilities as well as the pitfalls of a stage approach.

IV The Economic Interpretation of History Marx and Beard

Stephen Salsbury

THESE days reporters of the current American scene are constantly being urged to tell it like it is. For historians this is not a new concept, however much certain members of the younger generation would like to claim credit for the idea. Indeed this ideal smacks very much of early nineteenth-century Germany, for in the preface to his first work the historian Leopold von Ranke wrote these much quoted lines: "To history has been assigned the office of judging the past, of instructing the present for the benefit of future ages. To such high offices this work does not aspire: It wants only to show what actually happened."[1] But when the historian sits down at his typewriter to write it like it was, the task proves frustrating. The past, even a brief slice of it, cannot be re-created in all its terrifying complexity, and, even if it could, it would be beyond the comprehension of mortal man. In short, the human mind finds it necessary to focus on particular facts in order to make sense out of any event past or present. These facts are inevitably determined by the interest of the viewer.

History, therefore, is molded by the present because current environment shapes the kinds of questions historians ask of the past. It is not popular today in a world dominated by the scientist and the social scientist to admit that such subjective considerations shape our inquires into the past. Like Ranke we feel more comfortable with the myth that objectivity and detachment determine our scholarly efforts. Among the devices which historians invoke to generate the illusion of scientific precision, none is more popular than the model. This does not imply that the model is without merit. Indeed, I believe quite the contrary, but at the outset I wish to strip away the halo which gives to any model the appearance of analyzing the past in either objective or final terms.

In the last analysis models are useful only to the extent that we

[1]Quoted in Fritz Stern, *The Varieties of History* (Cleveland, 1956), 57.

realize their functions and, equally as important, their limitations. At the most elementary level the model is helpful because if it is carefully constructed it allows the historian to focus upon a particular problem and to select out of the past those facts that are relevant to his predetermined interest. At the most advanced level, historians, particularly those who have received their training in a social science such as economics, attempt to use models to test theories about human behavior. To rephrase Ranke, these writers attempt to study the past in order to derive historical laws which can be applied for the benefit of future ages. Thus a Rostow strives to discover the forces that move societies from a backward agricultural state to an advanced industrial condition.

But no matter how complex or carefully worked out, all historical models have one thing in common—they all deal with man. In so doing they make vital assumptions about human nature. Thus the model builder must answer certain questions about the human animal such as: Is he merely a complex mechanism responding to pressure from the outside environment? Or do deep inner drives such as those for food, procreation or security exercise a preponderent influence upon man's behavior? Psychologists and psychiatrists after much experimentation and study have yet to give us satisfactory answers to these problems. Most historical model builders, however, seldom make explicit the assumptions about human nature upon which their construction rests, and those who do never go much beyond making assertions about these matters. In short, a model is only as good as its analysis of the human animal; yet nearly all of effort in any model goes into marshaling historical facts that have but little bearing on this all-important question. In other words, one of the most vital things any historian must do before he sets pen to paper is to examine carefully his assumptions about human nature.

Having made these observations, I should now like to turn to the central theme of this essay, the economic interpretation of history. Assertions have already been presented here that sociologists like Max Weber were among the first model builders. It is probably fruitless to waste much time trying to find the first anything, especially when that first involves an intellectual concept, but suffice it to say that before Weber's birth year, 1864, Karl Marx and Friedrich Engels had already published their *Communist Manifesto*. This document, appearing in 1848, a year of political turmoil and revolution in Europe, was eventually followed by the first volume of *Das Kapital* in 1867. The *Manifesto* and *Kapital* set forth a model of historical change in which economic factors predominate.

The Marxist model appears in its starkest and briefest form in the *Manifesto*. It proclaims, "The history of all hitherto existing society is the history of class struggles. Freeman and slave, patrician and plebeian, lord and serf, guildmaster and journeyman, in a word, oppressor and oppressed, stood in constant opposition to one another, carried on an uninterrupted, now hidden, now open fight, a fight that each time ended, either in a revolutionary reconstitution of society at large, or in the common ruin of the contending classes."[2] At the root of this constant fight was the struggle for control of the means of production.

There are two aspects to this Marxist model that deserve consideration. The first is the assertion that economic conditions shape man's actions. To this I will return later. The second is the implication that the Marxist model not only describes past history in a meaningful way but also can predict the future. Marx viewed the bourgeoisie, the dominant force in his own day, as arising inevitably out of the class tensions which the feudal economy set in motion. And he predicted that tensions building between the capitalists and the workers in the nineteenth century would just as surely generate a revolution that would see the proletariat become victorious and the classless society arrive. Many of Marx's followers have seized upon his model as a vehicle to explain all history past and future. His detractors have made much of the fact that the predictive part of the doctrine, that is, the intensification of class warfare, revolution and the victory of the proletariat, neither has occurred nor seems imminent in the major industrial states of the Western world.

Marx himself, when looking back upon his writing, rejected the idea that his model was a universal explanation for all history. Writing in 1877 to a Russian journal published in Geneva, Marx explained some of the concepts he developed in *Das Kapital*:

The chapter on primitive accumulation does not pretend to do more than trace the path by which, in Western Europe, the capitalist order of economy emerged from the womb of the feudal order of economy. But that is too little for my critic. He feels he absolutely must metamorphose my historical

[2]Karl Marx and Friedrich Engels, *The Communist Manifesto*, ed. Samuel H. Beer (New York, 1955), 9.

sketch of the genesis of capitalism in Western Europe into a historico-philosophic theory of the general path every people is fated to tred, whatever the historical circumstances in which it finds itself, in order that it may ultimately arrive at the form of economy which ensures together with the greatest expansion of the productive powers of social labour, the most complete development of man. But I beg his pardon. He is both honouring and shaming me too much. Let us take an example.

In several parts of *Capital* I alluded to the fate which overtook the plebeians of ancient Rome. They were originally free peasants, each cultivating his piece of land on his own account. In the course of Roman history they were expropriated. The same movement which divorced them from their means of production and subsistence involved the formation not only of big landed property, but also of big money capital. And so one fine morning there were to be found on the one hand free men, stripped of anything except their labour power, and on the other, in order to exploit this labour, those who held all the acquired wealth in their possession. What happened? The Roman proletarians became not wage labourers, but a mob of do-nothings more abject than the former 'poor whites' in the South of the United States, and alongside of them there developed a mode of production which was not capitalist but based on slavery. Thus events strikingly analogous [to the nineteenth century] but taking place in different historical surroundings led to totally different results. By studying each of these forms of evolution separately and then comparing them one can easily find the clue to this phenomenon, but one will never arrive there by using as one's master key a general historico-philosophical theory, the supreme virtue of which consists in being super-historical.[3]

Marx is telling us that his model does little more than enable historians to focus their thoughts about the past in a meaningful manner. He does not claim for his efforts predictive power. This explains why Marx is so uncertain when he discusses the potentialities for socialist revolution in various countries in the nineteenth century. Will the revolution come first in England, Germany or Russia? Twice Marx suggests that it will take place in relatively underdeveloped countries. In 1847 he sees Germany as ripe for Communism, and in 1882 in a preface to the Russian edition of the *Manifesto* he suggests that Russia may see the first revolution. In the words of Shlomo Avineri, "Marx chooses the more underdeveloped countries not because they are not capitalistic at all (in such a case, of course, the term 'proletarian revolution' would have no meaning), but because

[3]Quoted in Shlomo Avineri, *The Social and Political Thought of Karl Marx* (Cambridge, Eng., 1968), 151–52, from Karl Marx, *Selected Correspondence, 1846–1895* (New York, 1942), copyright © 1942, reprinted by permission of International Publishers Co., Inc.

he feels that the late development of capitalism in these countries will promote two necessary processes simultaneously: a rapid development of a sophisticated capitalism and the concurrent intensive emergence of a proletariat. If this double pressure is too heavy, a society thus challenged may not be able to withstand it."[4] Whatever the case, the important fact is that Marx sees economic institutions not, for example, man's inner drives for security or procreation, shaping history. Is, therefore, the Marxian man merely a rather complex blob of protoplasm that responds primarily to the outside pressure of economic organization?

Many historians either Marxist or influenced by Marx's writings have answered yes to the above question and have rewritten history accordingly. The volumes flowing from these efforts have shaken the historical profession to its foundations. To illustrate this point I would like to turn to two examples.

Let us first consider the Middle Ages and the institution of feudalism. To many of us today, I suspect, the chapter on feudalism in the leading Marxist historian Maurice H. Dobb's *Studies in the Development of Capitalism* does not seem very revolutionary. Yet let us look more closely. Because of his devotion to Marx's ideas Dobb finds it imperative that he reformulate the very definition of the term *feudalism*. The emphasis of Dobb's definition lies "not in the juridical relation between vassal and sovereign, nor in the relation between production and the destination of the product, but in the relation between the direct producer (whether he be artisan in some workshop or peasant cultivator on the land) and his immediate superior or overlord." Dobb sees feudalism as a "mode of production" that is virtually identical with serfdom, which he defines as "an obligation laid on the producer by force and independently of his own volition to fulfill certain economic demands of an overlord, whether these demands take the form of services to be performed or of dues to be paid in money or in kind."[5]

Dobb's definition is no semantic quibble with previous historical writings. To see this we have only to turn to the traditional approach. Anyone who studied English constitutional history with Helen Maud Cam (to whom Dobb refers in his opening paragraph on fuedalism) or with Samuel Thorne is struck by the sharp conflict between

[4]*Ibid.*, 151.
[5]Dobb, *Studies in the Development of Capitalism* (New York, 1963), 35.

the two approaches. François Louis Ganshof, a scholar whom Thorne considers to be one of the most authoritative on the subject, says that feudalism "may be regarded as a body of institutions creating and regulating the obligations of obedience and service—mainly military service—on the part of a free man (the vassal) towards another free man (the lord), and the obligations of protection and maintenance on the part of the lord with regard to his vassal."[6]

Thus the traditionalist sees feudalism as primarily a military system. How does this differ from Dobb? Cam, Thorne and Ganshof see the feudal structure arising, not out of man's economic requirements, but in response to his basic need for security. Thus Ganshof looks for the beginnings of feudalism in the Merovingian Period which followed the collapse of the Roman Empire. Almost his first words are, "Under the Merovingians, Gaul was rarely united or at peace, and it frequently lapsed into a state of almost complete anarchy."[7] If pressed to elaborate upon his concept of the historical process, a traditionalist might assert that the force which shaped history was not the response to modes of production but man's inner psychological requirement for security and peace. In short, mankind constructs institutions to achieve these aims. To phrase this in terms that were common among certain politicians in the 1968 election year: law and order are necessary preconditions to the development of institutions that will guarantee racial equality. Whatever one might think of that idea, nobody can deny that it strikes a responsive chord in many Americans in these troubled times.

Now let us turn to a second example of the revolution in history caused by economic interpretation. If we survey all writings by American historians about the United States we can find no work that has caused more turmoil and set in motion more reevaluation of our past than Charles A. Beard's *An Economic Interpretation of the Constitution of the United States*, first published in 1913. Before we proceed further, one word of caution. It would be wrong strictly speaking to regard Beard's work as Marxian. Beard himself when writing in 1935 played down Marx. Said Beard, "Nor can I accept as a historical fact [the] . . . assertion that the economic interpretation of history or my volume on the Constitution had its origin in 'Marxian theories.' As I point out in Chapter I of my *Economic Basis of Poli-*

[6]Ganshof, *Feudalism* (New York, 1961), xx.
[7]*Ibid.*, 3.

tics, the germinal idea of class and group conflicts in history appeared in the writings of Aristotle, long before the Christian era, and was known to great writers on politics during the middle ages and modern times."[8] Beard confessed to being "conversant with the theories and writings of Marx."[9] But the historian also asserted that he drew his ideas from, among others, Machiavelli, Locke and Number 10 of the *Federalist Papers*, written by James Madison.

Regardless of where the ideas originated, however, it would be fair to say that when Beard wrote the *Economic Interpretation* he would have subscribed to the idea that past history can be most meaningfully explained in terms of class conflicts over property. This idea certainly shows Marx's influences, but there are important differences between the two men. Marx's man is shaped by institutions which come initially into being to enable man to produce goods. Thus Marx's man tends to be shaped by environment. Beard's man is motivated more by an inner desire to acquire and control property. Once Beard's man achieves economic dominance he erects institutions to perpetuate his position. And as conditions change Beard's man consciously creates new institutions to preserve his interests, that is, new forms of government such as the Constitution and new modes of production such as the industrial corporation. Beard certainly questions Marx's idea of the inevitable revolution or triumph of the proletariat. Unfortunately, Beard and his followers postulate a simplistic single-purpose man, a concept that does violence to reality. What is probably worse, Beard's thinking has produced a school of historians that views American history as the story of an economic elite which achieved dominance toward the end of the colonial period and which has successfully perpetuated itself in power almost to the present day.

Now let us return to *An Economic Interpretation of the Consitution of the United States*. Beard's purposes are clear enough. He set out to prove that the document resulted less from abstract feelings of patriotism than from the economic interests of those who wrote it. First Beard demonstrated that "four groups of property rights were adversely affected by the government under the Articles of Confederation, and that economic motives were behind the movement for a

[8]Beard, *An Economic Interpretation of the Constitution of the United States* (New York, 1954, xii.
[9]*Ibid.*, xiii.

reconstruction of the system." Next he asked the following questions: "Did the men who formulated the fundamental law of the land possess the kinds of property which were immediately and directly increased in value or made more secure by the results of their labors at Philadelphia? Did they have money at interest? Did they own public securities? Did they hold western lands for appreciation? Were they interested in shipping and manufactures?"[10] Then came Beard's key question: Did the Constitutional Convention "represent distinct groups whose economic interests they understood and felt in concrete, definite form through their own personal experience with identical property rights, or were they working merely under the guidance of abstract principles of political science?"[11] Of course Beard found that the men at the Philadelphia convention did indeed have the property interest which he found adversely affected under the Articles of Confederation.

The storm which the publication of *An Economic Interpretation* caused probably surprised even Beard. Objections came from two widely separated fronts. The first and most strident came from the legal profession, many of the judiciary and, of course, conservative men of property. In order to understand this reaction it must be realized that Beard published his volume in 1913 at the height of the progressive agitation against big business and the trusts. Throughout the latter part of the nineteenth century and into the beginning of the twentieth century the Supreme Court stood as a bulwark against attacks on big business. Through decisions such as the Minnesota Railroad Commission case of 1890, the Court struck down state laws that hindered business interests. And in the classic E. C. Knight case of 1895 the Sherman Anti-Trust Act was vitiated. Even the Court's support of Theodore Roosevelt's celebrated trust-busting did not panic big business. After all the Northern Securities decision of 1901 destroyed nothing; it merely prevented further concentration in a specific situation. And in the Court-ordered dissolution of the unpopular Standard Oil Company of New Jersey and the American Tobacco Company, both in 1911, the bench made clear in its "rule of reason" that most trusts need not fear its wrath. Later decisions, such as that in 1920 upholding the giant United States Steel Corpora-

[10]*Ibid.*, 73.
[11]*Ibid.*

tion's legality, confirmed that Wall Street could count upon a sympathetic ear from the Court.

From the progressive point of view the Court's behavior was particularly infuriating because it claimed to be merely upholding legal concepts embodied in the Constitution, a document all Americans knew was conceived in Philadelphia by disinterested, right-thinking patriots. And since the founding of the Republic, judges had taken care to establish the concept that the legal system stood apart from partisan political and economic considerations.

Because Beard stripped away the cloak of impartiality from the Constitution and by implication from the Supreme Court, he brought down upon himself disapproval, particularly from lawyers. Members of the New York Bar Association formed a committee and summoned him to appear before it. When Beard declined "on the ground that [he] . . . was not engaged in legal politics or political politics, they treated . . . [his] reply as a kind of contempt of court."[12] President Taft condemned the book. Beard's archenemy, Samuel Eliot Morison, gleefully quotes in "History by Innuendo," a subsection of his witty essay "History through a Beard," a letter written by Oliver Wendell Holmes to Sir Frederick Pollock.

Beard, said Holmes, argued "that the Constitution primarily represents the triumph of the money power over democratic agarianism and individualism. Beard . . . went into rather ignoble though most painstaking investigation of the investments of the leaders, with an innuendo even if disclaimed. I shall believe until compelled to think otherwise that they wanted to make a nation and invested (bet) on the belief that they would make one, not that they wanted a powerful government because they had invested. Belittling arguments always have a force of their own, but you and I believe that high-mindedness is not impossible to man."[13]

It is easy to see why men of the legal profession, who had a deep personal stake in maintaining the myth that the Constitution and the court system are above and apart from the real struggles within the American society, did not care to debate or even consider Beard's arguments on rational terms. More difficult to understand are the attacks directed at his book by leading members of the historical profession. Beard, in the introduction to the 1935 edition of his book, commented that irrational reactions were still continuing more than

[12]*Ibid.*, viii.
[13]Morison, *By Land and By Sea* (New York, 1954), 329.

twenty years after its publication. Beard noted Professor Theodore Clarke Smith's address before the American Historical Association in 1934, which asserted that the book illustrated a type of historical writing which is "doctrinaire" and "excludes anything like impartiality." Smith opined, "This is the view that American history, like all history, can and must be explained in economic terms. . . . This idea has its origin, of course, in the Marxian theories."[14]

Smith's attack enraged Beard, who proceeded to demolish it. Said Beard, "Now as a matter of fact there is no reason why an economic interpretation of the Constitution should be more partisan than any other interpretation. It may be employed, to be sure, to condemn one interest in the conflict or another interest, but no such use of it is imposed upon an author by the nature of the interpretation. Indeed an economic analysis may be coldly neutral."[15] Then Beard made light of Smith's concept that "the men who favored the Constitution were 'straight-thinking' men. Those who opposed it were 'narrower' men."[16] Beard felt that this theory "assumes that straight-thinking and national-mindedness are entities, particularities, or forces, apparently independent of all earthly considerations coming under the head of 'economic.' It does not say how these entities, particularities, or forces got into American heads. It does not show whether they were imported into the colonies from Europe or sprang up after the colonial epoch closed." According to Smith, concluded Beard, "whoever does not believe that the struggle over the Constitution was a simple contest between the straight-thinking men and narrower and local men of the respective sections is to be cast into outer darkness as 'Marxian' or lacking in 'impartiality.' Is that not a doctrinaire position?"[17]

It remained for the post–World War II period to produce historians who could criticize Beard at length using his own framework. Forrest McDonald's *We The People, The Economic Origins of the Constitution*, published in 1958, is the most thorough analysis of Beard's work in print. McDonald, unlike Theodore Smith, did not quarrel with the concept that economic factors can and do shape

[14]Beard, ix. Cf. Theodore Clarke Smith, "The Writing of American History, 1884 to 1934," *American Historical Review*, XL (April 1935), 477.

[15]*Ibid.*, ix.

[16]*Ibid.*, xi.

[17]*Ibid.*, x.

decision-making. To test Beard's thesis McDonald makes a detailed state-by-state analysis of the delegates to the Constitutional Convention and then the ratification procedures. Two salient facts emerge from this study. First, Beard's economic interest groups are too simple to reflect adequately reality in the 1780s. Second and more important, McDonald discovered that members of Beard's economic interest groups tended to support both sides of the question in substantial numbers. This rules out the idea that these groups spearheaded the drive for the adoption of the Constitution. In a summary statement McDonald concluded that

there were in the United States in 1787 at least twenty basic occupational groups having distinctly different economic characteristics and needs, and there were six basic forms of capital in addition to occupational activity. Most of the occupational groups and all the forms of capital may be divided into two to seventy-five subdivisions. Of the grand total of major economic interest groups and forms of investment, about 30 per cent were affected by the Constitution directly and immediately in a favorable way, and about 15 per cent were directly and immediately affected in an unfavorable way. The remaining 55 per cent were either not directly affected at all or were affected in indefinite, indecisive, or unpredictable ways.

McDonald points out that the numerous conflicts within these groups make it "not even theoretically possible to devise a single set of alignments on the issue of ratification that would explain the contest as one in which economic self-interest was the principal motivating force."[18] McDonald does not rule out an economic interpretation, but he insists that Beard's answers are not valid and that future study will have to be based upon an analysis of the behavior of the complex interest groups that actually existed.

Cold, hard, McDonald-like analysis has been applied on a wide front since the Second World War to much Beardian-oriented populist and progressive history. The result has been that Beard's simplistic economic man has fallen into disrepute. At the same time there has been a revival of interest in Marx, but with a change in emphasis.

The new view of Marx can be explained partly by the discovery and widespread circulation of two bodies of Marx's writings, *The German Ideology*, printed for the first time in 1932, and the

---

[18]McDonald, *We The People: The Economic Origins of the Constitution* (Chicago, 1958), 398.

Economic-Philosophical Manuscripts discovered the same year.[19]
These tracts have pushed thinking away from Marx's grand model
for history and back toward the place where all model building
should start, an analysis of the nature of man himself. It is not sur-
prising that scholars, like Erich Fromm, trained in psychoanalysis,
sociology and philosophy, rather than those trained in history or
economics, have taken the lead in this movement. What emerges out
of this is a view of man almost totally dominated by his economic
environment. Thus the major emphasis is not on the class struggles
which move men from one epoch to another such as from feudalism
to capitalism, but rather upon present capitalism. The central emphasis is upon man's alienation from his true nature, the result of
modern economic institutions. Thus Fromm can write, "Marx's central criticism of capitalism is not the injustice in the distribution of
wealth; it is the perversion of labor into forced, alienated, meaning-
less labor, hence the transformation of man into a 'crippled mon-
strosity.' "[20]

The popularity of such views in our own decade should come as no
surprise. This interpretation allows one to criticize the current economic structure without resorting to the discredited, simplistic
Beardian version of economic man. It also rings true for a generation that has seen many important movements not based on economic motivation spring up, such as that for civil rights. There is
something irresistible about a theory that maintains that most men
are alienated from their true condition and if we could but modify
our economic institutions man's warped ugly nature could be re-
formed.

Is the Marxian man who emerges from Fromm's pen a satisfactory model? First we might ask even if man is basically shaped by
environment are economic institutions the primary factors in that
environment? Men like David Donald and Richard Hofstadter talk
about status as a factor in shaping human actions. Status may find
expression through gradations of wealth, but in reality status implies a power relationship that exists even in societies where there
is little or no economic distinction between the various members.
And what shall we say of the inner forces that drive men? Can we dis-

[19]Avineri, 1.
[20]Fromm, *Marx's Concept of Man* (New York, 1961), 42.

regard the need to find security or peace of mind as a major factor in shaping man's actions? Fromm himself has written a book called *Escape from Freedom* based upon this very theme. These are questions which all of us must answer for ourselves as we sit down to write history. As much as I would like to, I cannot answer them for you.

V Toward a Useful Model for Social Change

Thomas C. Cochran

THE model discussed here has arisen not from a digest of existing theory but rather from a few initial hypotheses applied to a considerable body of data spread over many years.[1] I hope, therefore, that by presenting a plan based so largely on satisfying the data, we may find a basis for common agreement.

The difficulties that one encounters in pursuing the vast literature on social or economic change in the different disciplines are first, of course, differences in definition which may be partly overcome by a minimal use of technical language and, second, lack of focus on essential processes involved in change. Albert O. Hirschman, for example, has written, "It is not possible to identify a finite number of 'reliable' obstacles to development or a hierarchy among these obstacles which would permit us to arrange them neatly into boxes marked 'basic,' 'important,' 'secondary,' etc."[2] Obviously this remark applies equally to causes of economic development or other change. Hence the only hope for a simple model appears to lie in focusing sharply on universal and essential processes for which the factors of change serve as inputs.

Although many geographic, demographic, ideological and technological factors may initiate change, they become socially operative only as they influence human behavior, or still more precisely, as they lead to human decisions. Fortunately, there are well-accepted anthropological, psychological and sociological systems for analyzing and classifying decision-making. The model discussed here is built around role theory because, although this concept is

---

[1] I am indebted to Stanley Bailis for a survey of theories on social change in a thesis in preparation at the University of Pennsylvania. For general discussion, see Amitai and Eva Etzioni (eds.), *Social Change: Sources, Patterns and Consequences* (New York, 1964), and Wilbert E. Moore, *Social Change* (Englewood Cliffs, N. J., 1965).

[2] Hirschman, "Obstacles to Development: A Classification and a Vanishing Act," *Economic Development and Cultural Change*, XIII (July 1965), 385.

generally accepted in the behavioral sciences, it has been underexploited by students of social change in general, and particularly by economists. Roles are frequently mentioned in theoretical discussions of change but almost never used to their full explanatory limits. A role model focused entirely on the factors entering into a defined sequence of decisions also greatly facilitates cross-cultural and cross-temporal comparison. Another strength of role theory is that it substitutes researchable situational factors for deductive assumptions regarding uniformities of motivation.

A few years ago two able and well-intentioned sociologists edited a book on concepts and research in role theory.[3] Unfortunately, in the course of nearly four hundred double-column pages, buttressed by a 1,500 item bibliography, they and their associated authors were able to complicate and vary role theory and its definitions enough to place it securely in the hands of specialists, beyond the reach of chance intruders from other areas of knowledge. Because I have been an outsider from the start of role theory some three decades ago, I can substitute conventional English for technical language without feeling that I am committing treason against the disciplines of sociology and social psychology.

Presumably neither economists nor economic historians have any quarrel with efforts at systematizing the factors entering into decisions beyond those special cases dealt with in economic theory. As Bert F. Hoselitz remarks in the new *International Encyclopedia of the Social Sciences*, "On the purely analytical level the economic problems of economic development are relatively simple, but the political and social aspects of the process are more complex and elusive."[4] This problem of complexity is central. At first glance the following model will seem too simple, but it seems best in this case to have a general pattern that is simple enough to be kept in mind as a coordinate whole. Then the complexities and subtleties may be pushed into subcategories where they can, at least, be isolated if not explained or evaluated.

By definition roles are played to fulfill the functional demands of social positions or statuses. Each role is a series of connected deci-

[3]Bruce J. Biddle and Edwin J. Thomas (eds.), *Role Theory: Concepts and Research* (New York, 1966).
[4]Hoselitz, "Economic Growth: Non-Economic Aspects," *International Encyclopedia of the Social Sciences* (New York, 1968), IV, 423.

sions dependent on the social situation and the human actor. In other words, the utility of the model depends, first, on a categorization of the social forces bearing on the role players; and second, on the latter having some uniform characteristics that influence their responses. For the data with which I have worked, a model with three major categories has proved useful.

Since all categories are interconnected there can be no logical sequence of presentation. Arbitrarily I will start with the most elusive element, the types of personalities likely to be present among people undertaking a particular role. This may be broken down into the conditioning factors bearing upon childhood and youth in the culture which shape what may be termed character, as distinct from personality as a whole, and the individual's cognition of his environment. He sees the role in terms of desirable ends, or cultural values, modified by the habits and customs of his society. Proceeding with a brief over-all view of the model, the second major element is the resources in knowledge and social institutions available to the role player.[5] The third, and last, element is the sanctioning pressures brought to bear on the player by the groups involved in carrying out the anticipated role. These influential people have come, collectively, to be called the role-set, although, in a simpler stage of terminology, sociologists used the more descriptive phrase *defining groups*.

Social change occurs when, for whatever reason, an actor makes an innovation in role playing either accepted by his principal role-sets, and thereby establishing a new social norm of anticipated conduct, or setting in motion some chain of reactions on other roles that alter the anticipated relationships in the society. I will show the types of material that bear on each of the three major elements of the model from the data of American economic history. In general, while these illustrate values and situations favorable to economic change and development, they also suggest factors inimical to change. Furthermore, in contrast to so much of the theorizing about change that is in terms of the gross shifts from what are termed traditional societies to modern ones, these are illustrations of the subtler changes that take place in a society already modern.

[5]Wayne Broehl, in a paper soon to be published, has developed a roughly similar model, which lends support to the assumption that these elements result from analyzing the data of change.

The first major category of the model, depending on internal characteristics of the actor, is the hardest to fill from historical evidence. The adult is assumed to have a roughly ascertainable character resulting from the usual forces conditioning childhood and youth in his particular society. In some cases imperfect socialization may be present, the result of such causes as education in a dissident sect or migration from another culture. To learn all the different conditioning forces bearing on the youth of a society in any generation and the different strivings for identity that they produce is impossible. But where recruitment for a role brings to it people of the same general education, environment and social status, character becomes a hypothetically usable factor.

Take, for example, the successful American corporate executive of the late nineteenth century. Studies indicate that normally, or modally, he was reared in a religiously devout family whose head was in business in a town or city, and he was educated in a conventional secondary school. Perhaps a third or more such men attended college.[6] These measurable common elements plus indirect evidence regarding middle-class child-rearing practices provide a basis for generalizations regarding modal character.

But character is only one of the two major elements in present conceptions of personality. The other, cognition of the immediate environment, is associated with the social learning of the culture and the particular conditioning or socialization of the actor. Since men with similar learning and experience will tend to see the same aspects of their environment, some generalizations are possible regarding uniformities in this element. Hence, personality, which depends on the interplay of inward character and cognition of the outward situation, is, in turn, a variable subject to some limitations or assumptions as to modes.

The historian, in practice, usually heads into the analysis of personality from the opposite direction. In accumulating evidence he finds uniformities in response to certain situations, and these suggest some aspects of a modal personality. Applied to American entrepreneurs one can readily document characteristics such as high motivation for success, optimism, an emphasis on activity as a virtue in itself, as well as a number of other traits.

[6]See William Miller (ed.), *Men in Business* (Cambridge, Mass., 1952), 193–211, and Thomas C. Cochran, *Railroad Leaders* (Cambridge, Mass., 1953), 29, 220.

In a free society there is an initial question of whether on the basis of his cognition or perception of the situation a man wants to occupy the status to which an anticipated role is attached. His decision seems increasingly influenced by values, goals, or other cultural factors as societies become more economically developed. Anthropologist Evon Z. Vogt has written, "The importance of value orientation in shaping the direction of change is proportional to the economic and technological control a society has achieved."[7] Although the man's decision will depend, in large part, on the rewards to be hoped for from occupying a certain position, the nature of what is appealing as a reward will reflect the hierarchy of values and the institutional structure of the particular culture. Rewards may not be measured in economic values; their effectiveness or lack of effectiveness will depend greatly on the social statuses from which entrepreneurs are mainly recruited.

In many underdeveloped societies profit from a business venture may not be the ultimate goal. The entrepreneur's major aim may be social prestige, maintenance of his position as head of the family through providing employment for his kinship group or securing just enough money to take up some other type of life. In modern Europe and in the present-day United States it has often been difficult to keep successful entrepreneurial families devoted to business rather than to more prestigious but less remunerative activities. In sum, of every entrepreneur it has to be asked not only how high are his desires for achievement and how good are his economic prospects for success, but also what are his true reasons for undertaking the business? Empirical evidence suggests a subhypothesis that when economic roles are played for strictly economic goals results will be economically better than when such roles are played for ambigous or contradictory reasons.

In nineteenth-century America, for example, values tended to be established in the market place. Middle-class, materialistic values were widespread, or modal, and, therefore, regardless of the player's social origins, monetary gain was likely to be the immediate and compelling goal of entrepreneurial roles. This was true even of farmers who, before the late nineteenth century, were a majority of the population. They lacked the attachment to particular pieces

[7]Vogt, "On the Concepts of Structure and Process in Cultural Anthropology," *American Anthropologist*, LXII (Feb. 1960), 266.

of land shown by farmers in Europe and other less mobile nations of the world. A piece of property was regarded in America as a capital investment, to be improved and sold when the owner could get a good price. When, in 1900, the Census Bureau began to collect figures on length of residence, about five years on a given farm in the North Central area appeared normal. From the early days these mobile farmers tended to be economically rational or, in sociological language, neutral rather than affective. Extensive rather than intensive farming practices also illustrated a rational bias in American entrepreneurial or managerial roles toward saving of labor and lavish use of land or raw materials.

Until the end of the nineteenth century the combination of abundant natural resources and a relatively small but growing population that promised increasing returns from successful business ventures generated a multiplier effect. Social psychologists stress the importance of reinforcement, that is, success, as a role is played in giving the player both a feeling of increasing control over his environment and a wiser selection of future risks.[8] In more felicitous language Alec P. Alexander writes, "Entrepreneurial action motivated by high expectations leads to pleasant surprises and more entrepreneurship."[9] The reverse is equally true, and whichever pattern becomes established in a society is likely to persist.[10]

High returns on both entrepreneurial efforts and use of capital in America not only encouraged frugality, saving and investment in domestic development but also led to the allotment of more of the actor's time and energy to the rewarding role. Talcott Parsons and Edward A. Shils point out that "when systems of gratification and instrumentality are intertwined in the same concrete system of social roles that many of the factors that cause [or arrest, I might add] change emerge from this intertwining."[11] Many American businessmen never found anything else in life as gratifying as business, while many men in other cultures have been reluctant entrepreneurs.

[8]See David C. McClelland, *The Achieving Society* (Princeton, N. J., 1961), 238–39; John H. Kunkel, "Values and Behavior in Economic Development," *Economic Development and Cultural Change*, XIII (April 1965), 259 ff.

[9]Alexander, "The Supply of Industrial Entrepreneurship," *Explorations in Entrepreneurial History*, 2nd ser., IV (Winter 1967), 138.

[10]O. H. Mowrer, *Learning Theory and Behavior* (New York, 1960), 438–41.

[11]Parsons and Shils, "The Content of Roles," in Biddle and Thomas, *Role Theory*, 239.

The religious belief of many people that economic success was a sign of God's grace may have been an added factor in producing satisfaction from work, but in America it seems unnecessary in explaining the choice of statuses.

Throughout most of American history careers outside business have had a relatively weak appeal. The army, public service, the church and the learned professions, the great avenues for prestigious careers in the Old World, were of much less importance in the colonies or the United States prior to the twentieth century. Except in a few times and places, public service, the chief alternative that drew able youths away from business and economic pursuits in western Europe, provided a weak influence. Able Americans in the nineteenth century tended to avoid public service in order to devote themselves to more profitable ventures. Although in the earliest stages of new communities leading merchants, lawyers and manufacturers took part in local government in order to insure the economic success of the town, as soon as a city was well established and business activities had grown more time-consuming, the entrepreneurs turned public duties over to lesser men. This was the usual situation in both local and state government, at least down to the 1930s, and in many respects to the present day. A man who went into politics was generally looked upon by the business elite as second-rate as far as ambition and ability were concerned. In contrast, in Germany or in France a minor public office carried more social prestige than a major business position and consequently drew away from business some of the ablest entrepreneurs.

These considerations suggest that although high motivation for achievement is undoubtedly a stimulant to successful entrepreneurship, it may also impel men into nonentrepreneurial or economically wasteful careers, such as the military, if more prestige or more certain rewards lie in those directions.[12] Furthermore, in advanced societies literature of any type, from school readers to popular magazines, may stress achievement motivation for the very reason that it is thought to be declining.

Keeping these qualifications in mind, it is still significant that earlier American parents appear to have trained their children for economic success. A study of American school readers from 1800 on, using David C. McClelland's achievement motivation grid, a meas-

---

[12]See Shmuel Noah Eisenstadt, "The Need for Achievement," *Economic Development and Cultural Change*, XI (July 1963), 427.

urement by content analysis, indicates that there was increasing emphasis on achievement motivation from 1800 to 1890 and a falling off from 1890 to 1950.[13] At least up to the end of the nineteenth century there appears to have been increasing pressure on children at home, in school and in church for behavior that would lead to success in the world of business.

Turning from the assessment of the part played by values or goals to the second major category of the model, the resources available for successfully pursuing the role, we find a large amount of ascertainable factual data. There is, for example, the support that the institutional structure of the society gives both to recruitment and to expectations of success in a given role. Institutions such as well-developed money markets and banks open the door to entrepreneurial roles for men who are not capitalists, as well as offering greater chances for survival and expansion. Specialized business services such as advertising, legal advice, credit, transportation or accounting perform a similar function in guiding the decisions of the small or medium-sized entrepreneur, as do favorable laws and government policies. An economically advancing society, such as that in America, also spreads opportunity by continually creating new roles, generally available to the partially educated and ambitious.

Statements regarding expectations in various roles are often found in correspondence, or, in the light of history, the then current probabilities may be reconstructed. Such analyses can lead to setting up rank orders of elements such as availability of credit, auxiliary services and security for different types of business in various geographic areas.

The effects of an optimistic or almost unquestioning confidence in external security can be seen in most of our colonial and early national history. Here governments were created not by an aristocracy or a military group but largely by businessmen for business purposes. As Willard Hurst says in *Law and the Social Process*, "The institution whose functional needs and expressions had widest reflection in public policy was the market."[14] The common-law traditions, which were ultimately adopted by all of the states, were developed to insure reliable markets and to protect the ownership of private prop-

---

[13]Richard de Charms and Gerald H. Moeller, "Values Expressed in American Children's Readers, 1800–1950," *Journal of Abnormal and Social Psychology*, LXIV (Feb. 1962), 136–42.

[14]Hurst, *Law and the Social Process* (Ann Arbor, Mich., 1960), 89.

erty. Except among the Tories in the American Revolution and the Confederate leaders for a year or two toward the close of the Civil War, no real fear of loss from conquest or confiscation ever existed in this country. There are few other nations in modern history of which this can be said. By looking at the economic development, or nondevelopment, of Argentina or Brazil, for example, one can see the depressing effect of long-run uncertainty, in both cases primarily political.

Another type of resource for the role player is his share in the level and type of social learning of the particular culture. This is, of course, an immense category, which can be broken down into subdivisions such as factual knowledge and its interpretation, beliefs and their expression in systems of thought, customary attitudes and the insights they emphasize or preclude, and means of disseminating information to those who can use it. Historians dealing with changes in and transfers of ideas may use explanatory submodels that cannot be examined here. For the present over-all model, social learning at a particular time is a given or a parameter, but the extent to which any one entrepreneur shares in this learning is a function, in part, of his social class and type of education, as well as of the channels for flow of information in the society.

In considering this category some widely accepted hypotheses are useful. One advanced by both psychologists and anthropologists is that people see only what they have been conditioned to see, or as Goethe put it, "we see only what we know." Innovative responses will, therefore, lie within the bounds of the subjective construction, or the range and type of imagination fostered by the social learning. The new will represent some recombination of the elements the actor is prepared to perceive.[15] The outer limits of this theorem are not very important, as the permutations and combinations of hundreds of existing elements are for practical purposes infinite. Its useful bearing is that in the normal or middle range of construction the innovations are not random and will presumably follow existing patterns of the culture.

[15]See H. G. Barnett, *Innovation: The Basis of Cultural Change* (New York, 1953), 181 *ff.* Percy D. Warner, "Barnett's Innovation after Eleven Years," *Explorations in Entrepreneurial History*, 2nd ser., II (Winter 1965), 147–48; and Anthony F. C. Wallace, *Culture and Personality* (New York, 1962), 122–26.

Analysis of the writing of a number of similarly placed business entrepreneurs in several studies has indicated the availability, under certain conditions at least, of the material necessary to define the limits of the normal or model range of subjective construction, and therefore has also provided the means to understand the reason for entrepreneurial reactions in some historical situations.[16] Crude rank orders for certain types of response may be set up on the basis of geographic area and types of educational and occupational conditioning.

Without regard, however, to such fine distinctions, some general types of cases seem important for innovation. One is when the actor has learned the routine ways of the local culture imperfectly, or as the psychologist would say, he has acquired deviant learning-sets. This may result either from being brought up outside of the culture or from an eccentric conditioning or socialization. Both are aspects of the same process. A man like J. Pierpont Morgan, brought up as an aristocrat on a country estate and initially educated by private tutors, was essentially being conditioned outside the general American culture. Such entrepreneurs have beliefs or attitudes that may be out of tune with certain roles they are expected to play; this sets up what Leon Festinger has called "dissonance."[17] Conversely, dissonance can result from the functional needs of roles changing faster than general beliefs.

The more common aspect of imperfect socialization in American history, however, was that of migrants either from Europe to America, where the imperfections in socialization might be great, or from one region in the United States to another, where the differences might be subtle. But in either case the in-migrant, likely a young adult, might innovate in the very process of adjustment.[18] The other frequent cause for innovation is extreme specialization in education and imagination centered on limited aspects of the social learning, as illustrated by men like Edison or Ford. This is equivalent to saying that routine inventions and innovations usually arise from

[16]See Cochran, *Railroad Leaders*, 218–20; Cochran, *The Puerto Rican Businessman: A Study in Cultural Change* (Philadelphia, 1959), 117–32; and Cochran and Reuben E. Reina, *Entrepreneurship in Argentine Culture: Torcuato Di Tella and SIAM* (Philadelphia, 1962), 256–70.

[17]Biddle and Thomas, 328.

[18]Barnett, 87–89.

men who combine deviant knowledge with emotional fixation on certain processes.[19]

The type of social learning in a nation is, of course, the product of a wide range of factors such as economic opportunity, historical traditions and social and political systems. Socioeconomic factors such as the relations between land, labor, capital and technology, for example, are reflected in prevailing attitudes or cultural biases that strongly affect role playing or entrepreneurial decisions. Thus, a market is not a mechanism where supply is acted on by demand and price results automatically, but rather a meeting of human decision-makers, each with an inner conception or bias regarding the probable course of change in the situation. In the continental United States optimism regarding future demand has been a prevailing bias, leading to a continuous trend toward overcommitment; whereas in Puerto Rico pessimism, stemming from the limited possibilities of local markets, has produced a bias toward avoidance of risk.

Other elements favorable to economic and technological innovation have been present in American social learning. From an early date education had a strong utilitarian bias, reflected in commercial academies, business curricula and excessively practical engineering schools, while certain religious and aristocratic influences, which generally operate in a non- or anti-utilitarian direction, were weaker in America than in many other nations.

Social learning favorable to growth also resulted from initial settlement by Europeans from the areas with the most advanced technical knowledge—the Dutch, the English and the French Huguenots. In the early seventeenth century the Dutch ranked as the most technologically advanced people in the world, and the English and the French were next. By the early eighteenth century the English were forging ahead of both the Dutch and the French, and so was the number of English migrants to America. Hence, most of the immigrants to America had a background of life in the most advanced technological civilizations. Many brought with them, therefore, a relatively high level of practical social learning valuable for economic progress.

[19]See Everett M. Rogers, *Diffusion of Innovations* (New York, 1962), passim, including an extensive bibliography.

Another important element in American learning favorable to economic development was its use of the English language, for up to the last half of the nineteenth century Britain was the most technologically developed nation. Since few entrepreneurs in any nation could or would read technical literature except in their own tongue, Americans could learn from English engineering and scientific journals more readily than could people speaking other languages. It is striking, for instance, that the automobile developed in Germany and France without knowledge on the part of the Americans working in the same field, mainly because the American pioneers did not read these languages.

The language barrier, in earlier times particularly, put the international transfer of information in the hands of just a few carriers whom Wayne Broehl calls "information brokers." These were often salesmen or manufacturers' agents representing producers outside the culture. This speech barrier also meant that entrepreneurs tended to import specialists, when needed, only from the nations that could supply men speaking the proper language. When they could not do so the exchange of information was often quite unsatisfactory.[20]

A limitation in American social learning was also important—the weakness of traditional habits and customs. Fewer American entrepreneurs had what Thorstein Veblen called "trained incapacities," the inability to see certain opportunities because of customary or habitual barriers. Charles Henry Wilson has written in *England's Apprenticeship, 1603-1763*, "Always the forces of mobility and growth were balanced against the forces of inertia, the forces of enterprise with those of custom," whereas in America the traditional practices the emigrants brought with them were continually pressed against the eroding edge of the demand for practical utility.[21]

The third and last of the major categories of forces operating on the actor or decision-maker is pressure from people able to define or sanction the playing of the role, or the role-set. These are individuals or groups such as the customers of a salesman or the board of directors of a corporate executive. Roles and their role-sets comprise the operating mechanisms of social structure, and the role-sets determine what one must learn to be conventionally socialized. There will normally be several such groups associated with a role, and they

[20]See, for example, Cochran and Reina, 87, 260.
[21]Wilson, *England's Apprenticeship, 1603-1763* (London, 1965), 359.

may have different desires as to how the role should be played. Although they vary in their power to enforce their wishes, the actor normally tries to live up to the expectations of as many as possible of these groups and resorts to strategies to counterbalance or avoid averse sanctions.[22]

Such activity may in itself be a source of change, but in addition a developing society presents novel situations where the expectations of the role-set are relatively undefined, leaving the role loosely structured. Since in such situations the role player also lacks a precise conception of how to act, innovation is likely. As already noted, mass migration to a new area provides a cause for such uncertainties that lead to useful innovation.[23] Throughout American history, the rate of migration, both westward and from country to city—the highest rate among the modern nations—has been a stimulant to social change. The same conditions account for the greater likelihood of structural innovation in young rather than old industry, or more generally, the fact that stability breeds stability and change induces further change.

Consideration of comprehensive models such as this one built upon personality, values, perception and social structure have virtue as an intellectual operation apart from the paradigm's operational effectiveness. As Michael Polanyi has observed, "We can know more than we can tell," or readily conceptualize.[24] The building and the application of a model reorder our thoughts and provoke insights whose use may not be immediately evident. The human mind is a far more versatile instrument than the artifices we employ to aid it.

So far, at least, descriptive or categorizing devices such as the one just described appear to be the only way of explicitly approaching long-run, or historic, change. More precise mathematical contructs depending upon the segregation of selected variables seem likely to continue to prove less comprehensive and hence less realistic. Perhaps, as Loren C. Eiseley warns, "the wild reality always eludes our grasp," but a broad and flexible net may, at least, confine it sufficiently to permit examination and inference.[25]

[22]Robert K. Merton, "Instability and Articulation in the Role Set," in Biddle and Thomas, *Role Theory*, 282.

[23]See Barnett, 87–93.

[24]Michael Polanyi, *The Tacit Dimension* (Garden City, N. Y., 1967), 4.

[25]Eiseley, *The Unexpected Universe* (New York, 1969), 21.

VI The Statistical Approach
Fundamental Concepts as Applied to History

Robert E. Gallman

AT BASE, economics is concerned with material human welfare; history, with change over time. Economic history is a marriage of the two, and its practitioners are fundamentally engaged in describing and explaining historical variations in material welfare. This is true of both "traditional" and "new" economic historians. According to Fritz Redlich, the former deal with the development of economic institutions; the latter, with the processes taking place within institutions.[1] But these are proximate, not ultimate, concerns. Economic institutions are of interest chiefly as they affect economic performance and the distribution of the proceeds of economic activity.[2] Economic processes are studied for the same reasons. The forces that determine the allocation of resources, the distribution of income, the level of input utilization and the rate of growth of output affect human welfare and derive their significance from that fact.

It is in this sense that the concepts I will discuss—the concepts of the national accounts—deserve the designation "fundamental" given them in the title of this essay. The accounts are constructed around a central measure, called the national income or the net national product,[3] that is intended to describe the net proceeds of the economic activity engaged in by the factors of production (land, labor, capital, enterprise) owned by a society. A society's only source of material well-being, apart from conquest, gifts or borrowings, is the supply of commodities and services produced by the

---

[1]Redlich, " 'New' and Traditional Approaches to Economic History and Their Interdependence," *Journal of Economic History*, XXV (Dec. 1965), 482.

[2]I do not wish to be dogmatic. The development of an economic institution may be studied, for instance, in relation to the distribution of political or social power, in which case the question of material welfare enters into the matter only obliquely.

[3]See Simon Kuznets, *Economic Change* (New York, 1953), chs. 6 and 7, especially 192–97. I treat the terms as equivalent, following the practice of Kuznets and the National Bureau of Economic Research. In the accounts of the U. S. Department of Commerce, the two are not identical. See National Bureau of Economic Research, Conference on Income and Wealth, *A Critique of the United States Income and Product Accounts*, Studies in Income and Wealth, XXII (Princeton, N.J., 1958).

factors owned by its members, individually and collectively. Thus the measurements composing the national accounts go to the heart of economic history. Whenever an economic historian writes that an economy was "flourishing" or "stagnating" or "in decline" or "farther advanced than a decade previously" or "at a peak not achieved for another decade," he is saying something about the economic performance of a society, and his statement could be cast in terms of the national accounts. When an author characterizes an event or institution as economically important or unimportant he is presumably describing an impact on the material well-being of the members of a society, which could be stated as a change in national income, in income per capita or in the distribution of income. All such descriptions are quantitative in nature, whether they are given precise numerical expression or not. The chief virtues of a properly defined numerical statement are that it is unambiguous and subject to test.

The national accounts represent a consistent system that describes not only the net proceeds of economic activity but also the magnitudes of theoretically interesting components of the national income and the national stock of wealth. The national income can be conceived of as the sum of net income flows to factors of production. Or one may consider the disposition of income and treat the national income as the sum of expenditures on consumables (perhaps distinguished by type) and net investment (savings), in which case the link between national income and the national wealth stock is made explicit. The income and expenditure measurements constitute separate views of the same aggregate. A highly articulated set of accounts provides a wealth of evidence by means of which the structure of the economy may be described and explanatory models may be tested. More generally, a knowledge of the structural details provides the economic historian with a valuable perspective on the economy, giving him a sense of proportion. Needless to say, the structural details distinguished are limited only by scholarly interests and resources and the supply of data.

II

So far I have dealt in general terms with the national accounts and the uses to which they can be put in the study of economic history. A description of this kind, removed from the particular, cannot properly convey the practical uses of the national accounts nor the problems encountered in income estimation and interpretation. Perhaps this deficiency can be made good if I now take up in some detail a piece of research in which income estimates are central, research reported in two papers by Paul A. David.[4] I have several objectives in mind. First, I think the David essays are imaginative and valuable contributions, demonstrating how much can be learned from just a few data. They are worthy models for study. Second, in this work David ventures into terra incognita, as he himself points out. The estimates he produces cry for further testing, and I would like to illustrate my previous comments by attempting some simple tests. Finally, I have so far made no mention of the interpretive problems posed by national income estimates. The David essays can serve as vehicles for discussion of the chief interpretive problems.

David's immediate objective is to measure the pace of economic change in the United States in the four or five decades before 1840. His ultimate objective is to demonstrate the value of a particular approach to the study of this country's economic growth. He believes that growth can be best understood if it is conceived of as a series of long upward surges, each followed by a long period of slower growth. The swings involved typically run from fifteen to twenty years, from peak to peak or trough to trough. An analysis based on such long undulations can only be tested satisfactorily against a record extending over many decades; this is one reason why David wants to extend the existing time series backward to the beginning of American national history.

A second and perhaps more compelling reason lies in the peculiar interest of the decade of the 1840s. According to Walt W. Rostow, the 1840s was the time of American "take-off," a period during which the economy experienced a fundamental change of trend. Although this interpretation has received heavy criticism, it has also won many adherents. And it is true that the existing aggregate product series

[4]David, "The Growth of Real Product in the United States before 1840: New Evidence, Controlled Conjectures," *Journal of Economic History*, XXVII (June 1967), 151–95. A shorter version of this paper appears as "New Light on a Statistical Dark Age: U.S. Real Product Growth before 1840," *American Economic Review*, LVII (May 1967), 294–306. A technical appendix to the *J.E.H.* paper was produced as "Memorandum No. 53A," Research Center in Economic Growth, Stanford University, Stanford, Calif., mimeographed (Dec. 1966).

shows that the rate of growth in the latter 1840s and early 1850s was unusually high. David's position is that this record probably reflects a long swing, not a long-term acceleration. But he quite properly points out that the nature of the experience of the 1840s cannot be fully appreciated until we know what went before. If Rostow has correctly identified the watershed of modern American growth, then the long-term pace of change prior to 1840 must have been relatively slow. The only way to test Rostow's theory is to produce acceptable measurements covering the preceding four or five decades because only in this way can we distinguish between long-term and long-swing rates of change. David finds the existing estimates for the years before the mid-1830s unacceptable, with good reason, and he is thus obliged to produce new ones.

Economic growth is commonly measured as the long-term rate of change in real national income (or net product) per capita. Economics is concerned with human material welfare, and therefore the growth of an economy should be measured by the increase in its ability to supply goods and services to its members. At issue is the output of the economy. For this reason price changes across time should not affect the measure; prices should be held constant so that they record changes in real output only. Furthermore, the ability of a society to provide a continuously more abundant material life for its people depends upon output growth proceeding at a more rapid pace than population growth. Therefore economic growth is typically measured in per capita terms.[5]

David's theoretical interests and his estimating constraints lead him to work with per capita domestic product (output produced by domestic factors of production) rather than the more conventional national product (output produced by factors owned by nationals). He also chooses the concept gross of capital consumption. For some economies across some stretches of time gross domestic product and net national product may have grown at quite different rates. But this was not true of the United States in the early nineteenth century. Domestic and national product were almost identical, and the share of product taken by capital consumption was typically limited.[6] Conse-

[5]Some shortcomings of the per capita measure are discussed below.

[6]See David, "Growth of Real Product," 168, and Lance E. Davis and Robert E. Gallman, "The Share of Savings and Investment in Gross National Product during the 19th Century, United States of America," in *Proceedings of the Fourth Congress of the International Economic History Association,* forthcoming.

quently, David's series, in so far as it is accurate, can serve as a good general index of growth.

The per capita real product figures (prices of 1840) implied by David's work are contained in Table 1. The rates of change computed from them appear to reflect long swings, and the average rates are not

TABLE 1. Real gross domestic product (prices of 1840) per capita in the United States, 1790–1840

	Variant I	Variant II
1790	—	$50
1800	$55	58
1810	52	56
1820	58	61
1830	74	76
1840	91	91

SOURCES: 1790: Per capita GDP in 1840 multiplied by .55 (Paul A. David, "Growth of Real Product in the United States before 1840: New Evidence, Controlled Conjectures," *Journal of Economic History*, XXVII [June 1967], 187, n. 69).

1800–1840: Per capita GDP in 1840 multiplied by the index numbers in David, 184, Table 8.

1840: GDP (David, 168, Table 5, col. 3, line 1) divided by population (U.S., Bureau of the Census, *Historical Statistics of the United States, Colonial Times to 1957* [Washington, D.C., 1960], Series A-2, 1840).

materially lower than those experienced in the decades just before the Civil War. The estimates therefore support David's position and refute Rostow's. I want to pursue two questions with respect to these figures: (1) Are they plausible? (2) How valid are the procedures by which they were produced? Let me consider each in turn.

III

The plausibility of a set of figures depends upon the degree to which they correspond with our expectations, which in turn are formed by knowledge of evidence of various kinds. I do not propose to make anything approximating a thorough canvass of independent evidence by means of which David's results may be judged. I have in mind a rather simple, incomplete, but nonetheless useful test. According to the basic 1840 estimate accepted by David, half of the gross domestic product (GDP) was composed of goods described as consumer perishables. Perishables at that date consisted almost exclusively of food and firewood.[7] Now a priori one would suppose that American standards of food and fuel consumption changed little across the half century before 1840. But if this is the case, David's per capita real product estimate for 1790, and probably those for 1800 and 1810 as well, is implausibly low, and therefore his computed long-term rate of growth is unrealistically high. For example, if the real value of per capita consumption of perishables remained entirely constant between 1790 and 1840, then the level achieved in 1790 was $45. But this figure represents nine-tenths of David's per capita GDP estimate at that date. Only one-tenth, or $5, is left for all other components of product, a result which is not acceptable. I propose to test David's results, therefore, by testing the proposition that per capita consumption of perishables changed little in the five decades before 1840. If the proposition survives the test, then there is some reason for supposing that David's computed rate of change of real product per capita overstates actual United States growth from 1790 to 1840, and his case against long-term acceleration is weakened.

Let me begin with cordwood consumption, since we have some comprehensive data on this component of GDP. According to the Forest Service, per capita cordwood consumption remained roughly constant over the half century before 1840.[8] The estimates are imperfect, and the level they describe at each date may very well be too high. But the trend across time is more important for present purposes than the level at any given date, and the trend is probably accurately depicted.[9] The estimates take into account the effects on consumption of changes in the regional distribution of population, supplies of standing timber and types of heating and cooking devices in use. There can be little doubt that they are adequate for present purposes. According to the 1840 estimate accepted by David, the value of firewood con-

[7]See National Bureau of Economic Research, Conference on Research in Income and Wealth, *Output, Employment and Productivity in the United States after 1800,* Studies in Income and Wealth, XXX (New York, 1966), 26, 27, 46, 47. The date 1839 in this source refers to census year 1839, which includes part of calendar years 1839 and 1840. In this paper I refer to the census year as 1840.

[8]Robert V. Reynolds and Albert H. Pierson, *Fuel Wood Used in the United States, 1630–1930,* U.S.D.A. Circular no. 641 (Feb. 1942). See also, Sam H. Schurr and Bruce C. Netschert, *Energy in the American Economy, 1850–1975,* Resources for the Future, Inc. (Baltimore, 1960), 45–57. The population data that infer per capita consumption are from U.S., Bureau of the Census, *Historical Statistics of the United States, Colonial Times to 1957,* Series A-2 (Washington, D. C., 1960).

[9]See Studies in Income and Wealth, XXX, 31–33.

sumed in the home came to $7 per head.[10] On the basis of the Forest Service evidence, per capita consumption at each of the earlier benchmark dates can also be taken to be $7.

Testing the proposition as it relates to food consumption is a more difficult matter. The real value, i.e., value in constant prices, of per capita food consumption varies with the composition of the population and the underlying consumption standards. Let me consider each briefly.

Assuming that underlying consumption standards remain constant, changes in the composition of the population affect per capita consumption in so far as various groups in the population follow different standards. For example, in the early decades of the nineteenth century, the fraction of the population represented by adults and the fraction represented by free men rose. Since adults consumed more food per head than children and free men had a better diet than slaves, these shifts in the composition of population must have tended to raise the level of average per capita food consumption. Now such developments are really irrelevant to the measurement of economic growth. The fact that a child eats more as he grows older does not mean that he is becoming better off in material terms. The shift in the distribution of the population between slave and free could be regarded as having an important positive effect on human welfare only if it arose out of manumission, which it did not. The increased per capita consumption flowing from these changes in the composition of population cannot be interpreted as a gain in material well-being and therefore should not affect the measure of economic growth. The general lesson to be learned from these examples is that per capita product is an imperfect index of economic performance. But it remains the best single, readily calculated measure, and David's decision to use it in his work cannot be seriously criticized. In any case, at this stage I am concerned with the plausibility of David's results, rather than their conceptual warrant. My test must therefore be made on David's terms, which require that

[10]See *ibid.*, 47, for the value of firewood consumption in 1840 (census year 1839) and *Historical Statistics* for the population estimate. David, "Growth of Real Product," 168, believes that the firewood figure "implies a somewhat overstated level of per capita use which makes it a suitable measure of all nonmineral fuel consumption."

the effect of demographic compositional changes on per capita consumption be calculated.

In addition to the two compositional changes discussed above, there is one more that must be taken into account.[11] Between 1790 and 1840 the share of population living in urban places rose from about 5 percent to about 12 percent. According to Ezra C. Seaman, food costs in the cities ran about 50 percent above those in the countryside, the difference being accounted for by distribution costs.[12] The drift to the cities therefore raised the value of per capita food consumption. So far as the measurement of growth is concerned, the increase is spurious. Real income (product) is supposed to represent the net proceeds of economic activity. The distribution expenses occasioned by urban life are not a net increment to material well-being but a cost of a particular form of organization. City organization led to improved productive efficiency, of course, but these results made themselves felt in higher levels of net output and are therefore reflected in the na-

[11]The distribution of the population by sex, region of residence, ethnic background and income are other possibilities. However, the sex composition of the population changed very little across time. The evidence of the militia rations, discussed below, suggests that regional variations in diet were not great. It seems doubtful that shifts in the ethnic composition of the population or the distribution of income caused substantial changes in per capita food consumption, but I have no data upon which to test the theory.

[12]Seaman, *Essays on the Progress of Nations* (New York, 1852), 278. Seaman's book contains remarkable estimates of components of national product. Some of the calculations underlying Tables 2 and 3 depend upon Seaman's work, since the published estimates used by David are not available in the required detail. The two sets of estimates appear to be quite different but are readily reconciled. According to Seaman, 278–83, the value of perishables consumed per capita in 1840, exclusive of fuel, came to $23.70 (food, tobacco, lighting, soap, books and periodicals, less items produced in the home). The figure underlying David's work is $38 (see Table 2, col. 5, line 6). The chief factors accounting for the difference between the two values appear to be as follows:

a. Seaman's prices of farm-produced foods are averages for the years 1840–45, whereas David's prices refer to census year 1839 (see n. 7). Since prices fell sharply in the early 1840s, Seaman's prices tend to be lower than census year prices (see, e.g., *Historical Statistics*, Series E-2 and E-3).

b. Seaman valued all farm-produced foods in *farm* prices of *unprocessed* foods, whereas the estimates employed by David allow for both processing and distribution.

c. Seaman's estimate of meat consumption by free men is lower than the figure implied by the estimates David uses (see n. 18).

There are other minor differences between the two sets of estimates. For purposes of the calculations underlying Tables 2 and 3, the Seaman estimates are adequate proxies for the figures composing the estimates underlying David's work.

tional product, exclusive of the additional distribution expense. The rise in distribution expense incident to urbanization is a cost of this increase and should be netted out of national product.[13] But David's estimating procedures probably do not accomplish this result. His series probably does reflect the changing cost of distribution associated with urban growth, and therefore my test must take into account the effects of the rural-urban shift on the value of food consumption.

Table 2 contains index numbers that describe the effects of each of the three demographic changes on the level of per capita food consumption. The estimates underlying these indexes are imperfect (see the notes to the table) but are adequate for present purposes. Column 4 shows the combined effect of all three changes in index number form, while column 5 gives the same information expressed in the form of money values (1840 prices). Column 5 shows that the level of consumption would have risen just $3.00, or less than 10 percent, had dietary standards remained constant and the level of consumption been affected only by changes in the structure of the population.

Let me now turn to the underlying consumption standards. According to Kenneth M. Stampp, a common slave ration schedule was followed throughout the slaveholding states. There was no systematic variation by region or by size or type of productive operation.[14] There is a good deal of evidence in support of Stampp's position.[15] The basic diet consisted of cornmeal and pork. Some supplements were given, the types depending in some measure on local resources and crops. But the literature suggests no long-term improvement or deterioration in standards across time.

I have not made a careful search for evidence bearing on the diets of free men, contenting myself with readily available data. The most interesting figures I have come across are from the ration schedules of the colonial militia, colonial privateers and the Continental Army.[16] Schedules are available at various dates from the late seventeenth century through the Revolution and they relate to both north-

[13]See the exchanges between Richard A. Easterlin and George Jaszi in Studies in Income and Wealth, XXII, 133–38, 143–45.

[14]Stampp, *The Peculiar Institution* (New York, 1956), 282, 284.

[15]See Robert E. Gallman, "Self-Sufficiency in the Cotton Economy of the Antebellum South," *Agricultural History*, XLIV (Jan. 1970), 5–23, sections 2 and 4.

[16]*Historical Statistics*, 755, 774.

TABLE 2.   Effects of changing population structure on per capita food
consumption, 1790–1840 (1840 = 100)

	Indexes of demographic changes			Per capita food consumption	
	Free-Slave	Adult-Child	Rural-Urban	Col. 1 × col. 2 × col. 3	Col. 4 in terms of value (1840 prices)
1790	96.9	97.8	97.3	92.2	$35
1800	97.5	97.3	97.7	92.7	35
1810	97.8	97.3	98.3	93.5	36
1820	98.2	98.2	98.3	94.8	36
1830	98.7	99.1	99.0	96.8	37
1840	100.0	100.0	100.0	100.0	38

SOURCES: Col. 1: These figures are based on calculations shown in the following
table:

	Total pop. (in 1,000's)	Slave pop.	Free pop.	Col. 2 × .333 plus col. 3	Col. 4 divided by col. 1	Col. 5 as index on base 1840
1790	3,929	698	3,231	3,464	.882	.969
1800	5,297	894	4,403	4,701	.887	.975
1810	7,224	1,191	6,033	6,429	.889	.978
1820	9,618	1,538	8,080	8,592	.893	.982
1830	12,901	2,009	10,892	11,562	.897	.987
1840	17,120	2,487	14,633	15,462	.909	1.000

The distribution of the population between slave and free was computed from U.S.,
Bureau of the Census, *Historical Statistics of the United States, Colonial Times
to 1957* (Washington, D.C., 1960), Series A-2, -100, -107, -114. According to Ezra
C. Seaman, *Essays on the Progress of Nations* (New York, 1852), 278–83, the per
capita food consumption of free persons and house servants in 1840 had a value just
over $23.50, exclusive of the cost of processing and distributing farm-produced
foods. Seaman's estimate is probably $2 to $4 too low (see text, n. 18, and Seaman,
278, price of beef and pork), because of an inadequate meat consumption estimate,
if for no other reason. According to Seaman, the value of food consumption of the
typical field slave came to $12.50 per capita in the same year. If due allowance is
made for the lower consumption levels of slave children and for the downward biases
in Seaman's estimates of consumption by free persons, the value of a typical slave
diet would probably come to about one-third the value of a typical free diet (see
n. 12). I therefore gave the slave component of the population a weight one-third
as large as the weight of the free component when I computed the index numbers.
Specifically, I multiplied the slave population at each date by .333, added it to the
free population, divided through by the *actual* total population at each date, and
expressed the resulting series as index numbers on the base 1840 by dividing the
series through by the 1840 value and multiplying by 100.

Col. 2: I assumed the diet of a child under 15 typically cost one-half as much as an adult diet (see text and n. 19), and I computed the index numbers following the procedure used for col. 1 above. I assumed that the age distribution of white males adequately represented the age distribution of the total population and therefore based my estimates on the data in *Historical Statistics*, Series A-71-84, "male." The *Historical Statistics* data are not comparable from one date to the next. Consequently, I had to produce comparable estimates by interpolation:

	Under 15	Over 15
	(in 1000's)	
1790	763	852
1800	1,055	1,140
1810	1,433	1,555
1820	1,866	2,132
1830	2,425	2,938
1840	3,174	4,082

Col. 3: The distribution of the population between rural and urban was taken from *Historical Statistics*, Series A-195 and -206. I assumed with Seaman (see text and n. 12) that urban food costs exceeded rural by 50 percent. I computed the index numbers by the procedure used for col. 1 above.

Col. 5: 1840: Per capita consumption of perishables (see n. 7). 1790–1830: value for 1840 ($38) multiplied by index numbers in col. 4.

ern and southern colonies. The militia were citizen soldiers, not an elite corps or a group of hired ruffians, and presumably therefore the rations could not have deviated markedly from the standards typically followed by the soldiers in private life. Any fundamental changes across time in dietary practices ought to be captured in the schedules.

The most striking finding that emerges from the evidence is that the basic meat and bread ration varied scarcely at all across time, space and form of military organization. Soldiers and sailors typically received a pound of meat or fish and a pound of bread or flour per day. This standard applied to the North and South, at the end of the eighteenth century as well as the end of the seventeenth. Furthermore, there is reason to believe that the pattern of consumption persisted well into the nineteenth century. According to Seaman, around 1840 free men and house servants consumed about 150 pounds of meat and the wheat equivalent of between 200 and 250 pounds of bread per year.[17] The meat estimate is generally regarded as too low, per-

[17]Seaman, 278, asserts that consumption of wheat and flour amounted to four bushels per head, presumably in wheat equivalents. Four bushels of wheat can be converted into almost 250 pounds of hard bread, hard rolls or biscuits, almost 270 pounds of white bread, or over 170 pounds of pilot bread or hardtack, according to U.S., Production and Marketing Administration, *Conversion Factors and Weights and Measures for Agricultural Commodities and Their Products* (Washington, D. C., May 1952), 38.

haps by as much as 50 or 100 pounds,[18] and consequently it is likely that meat and bread were consumed at approximately the same rates, just as they were in colonial times.

The levels of per capita consumption of these two basic foods may also have changed little across time. According to the plantation day-books, adult female slaves typically received two-thirds of an adult male food ration; children, one-half of an adult ration. These coefficients are similar to ratios of required caloric intake appearing in modern dietary manuals and may therefore be appropriate means by which to infer typical consumption levels of colonial women and children from the evidence of the military schedules.[19] I have made

[18]The estimates of Marvin W. Towne and Wayne D. Rasmussen imply that per capita production of beef, veal and pork came to roughly 270 pounds net weight in 1840 (National Bureau of Economic Research, Conference on Income and Wealth, *Trends in the American Economy in the Nineteenth Century*, Studies in Income and Wealth, XXIV [Princeton, N.J., 1960], 283, 284). Towne and Rasmussen report live weights, which I have converted to net weights, at the rate of .75 for pork and .55 for veal and beef (see Gallman, "Self-Sufficiency in South," notes to Table 5; I took the population estimate from *Historical Statistics,* Series A-2, 1840). Correction for net exports would change this value little. Since slaves consumed less meat per capita than free men (for example, see Gallman, "Self-Sufficiency in South," Table 5 and related text), the Towne and Rasmussen estimates probably imply consumption by free men of more than 270 pounds and perhaps as much as 280 pounds. But Parker believes that the Towne and Rasmussen figure is too high (Studies in Income and Wealth, XXIV, 284, editor's footnotes), and it is true that the estimates underlying the 1840 GNP figure accepted by David imply a lower level of consumption (Studies in Income and Wealth, XXIV, 46–49, XXX, 56 and the sources cited therein), perhaps below 220 pounds for free and slave together. See also Gallman, "Self-Sufficiency in South," section 4, where a case is made that a figure of 225 pounds for free persons in 1860 is probably an upper bound. For 1840, the figure could have been somewhat higher, and the range 200–250 pounds probably includes the actual level.

[19]For example, the Wilkins Papers, Northampton County, North Carolina, Dec. 1862, Southern Collection, University of North Carolina Library, contain a corn ration of $1\frac{1}{2}$ pecks a week for adult male field hands, whereas women working in the fields were allotted one peck. Children under 2 were given no separate ration; those 2 to 9 received $\frac{1}{2}$ peck and those working in the fields, presumably over 9, 1 peck. Lewis C. Gray is the authority for the statement that children averaged half an adult ration *(History of Agriculture in the Southern United States before 1860* [Washington, D.C., 1933], I, 563). The Wilkins schedule probably implies a somewhat lower average, given the probable age distribution of the children. The modern caloric requirement for a male 154 pounds at heavy work is 4,500 calories; a woman 123 pounds, 3,000 (Ralph W. Gerard, *et al., Food for Life* [Chicago, 1952], 158). The margin narrows at less intense levels of activity, 2,400 and 2,000 in sedentary occupations. For present purposes, however, the comparison should be made at levels of hard physical work, since the populations I am discussing were

these calculations and have used the resulting figures to compute the per capita consumption of bread and meat that *would have taken place in 1840 had colonial standards been in effect at that time.* Specifically, I have weighted the free population components in 1840 with the colonial per capita bread and meat consumption relevant to each group and have calculated average consumption for all free men. The results I have obtained, 237 pounds of meat and 237 pounds of bread per head per year, are very close to the estimates based on Seaman's work described above, 200 to 250 pounds of meat and 200 to 250 pounds of bread.[20] There is some reason for believing, then, that standards of consumption of the basic items of diet, meat and bread, were essentially unchanging from the end of the seventeenth century to 1840.

It is more difficult to speak with confidence of the remaining elements of diet. Some of the colonial ration schedules mention only meat and bread; others list numerous supplements. Presumably the meat and bread schedules do not describe the full diet of the soldiers involved, but there is no way of knowing how complete the full diet was in these cases.[21]

---

typically engaged in such work. Gerard's schedules for children (159) call for between 110 calories for infants under 1 year and 3,200 calories for boys, 13–15 years. Assuming the typical colonial adult required around 3,750 calories a day, the typical child probably required somewhat less than half this value, since younger age groups were likely to be more numerous than older ones. But for present purposes, an allowance of one-half is accurate enough.

[20]According to the notes to Table 2, col. 3, about 43.7 percent of the free population in 1840 was under 15 years of age. In *Historical Statistics*, Series A-34, -35, -60, and -66, 51.0 percent of the free population was male. I therefore infer the following distribution: adult males, 28.7 percent; adult females, 27.6 percent; children, 43.7 percent. Men consume 365 pounds of meat and 365 pounds of bread per year, women two-thirds as much, and children half as much as adults. Therefore, average per capita consumption of each food equals:

$$365(.287 + .667 \times .276 + \left(\frac{.287 + .667 \times .276}{\frac{.287 + .276}{2}} \right) \times .437)$$

equals: 365 (.287 + .667 × .276 + .410 × .437)
equals: 365 (.287 + .184 + .179)
equals: 365 (.650)
equals: 237.

[21]Incidentally, the supplemented schedules do not cluster toward the end of the period; the evidence of the schedules provides no secure basis for hypothesizing an improvement in diet during the eighteenth century.

The ration list promulgated in 1775 for the Continental Army is the most complete of the group in that it contains the widest variety of food types. It is also most relevant for my purposes, since it applies to a time not far removed from the beginning of the period in which David is interested. I have therefore chosen to compare the pattern of that schedule with the pattern of consumption in 1840, as reported by Seaman. I have valued the 1775 list in prices of 1840 and have partitioned the results for that date and for 1840 among food groups. The results appear in Table 3. Of course, the 1775 figures refer to adult male consumption; the 1840 figures, to consumption of all free persons and house servants. Consequently, one cannot expect to pick up minor shifts in underlying standards by a comparison of these data. But perhaps major shifts can be identified. In particular, if diet improved between 1775 and 1840, one would expect to find that meat and grains, the basic items being consumed at approximately the same per capita rates at each date, declined in relative importance across time. In fact, no such change appears in the table. Indeed, the details of the table are remarkably similar at both dates. Such differences as do appear may reflect no more than the failure of the military schedule to capture the full range of colonial consumption. For example, the army ration does not mention eggs or fruit, although presumably these items were consumed in colonial times, if not in large amounts.

The relative stability of the structure of diet before 1840 is underlined by the entries in the last two columns of Table 3. These entries describe the composition of diet in 1909 and 1948, and they show marked differences from the figures in the first two columns. The full table suggests that standards of comsumption were virtually unchanging between 1775 and 1840 and that sometime between the latter date and 1909 they began to undergo important revision. Furthermore, the underlying data show that the shifts were in the direction of more expensive foods. The value of per capita consumption rose by about one-third between 1840 and 1909 and by about one-half between 1840 and 1948 (valuations in farm prices of 1840). That is, the data underlying Table 3 yield no evidence of growth before 1840, but substantial evidence of growth thereafter.

The data suggest that dietary standards changed little from colonial times to 1840. Therefore whatever changes took place in per capita food consumption were probably limited to those arising out of

TABLE 3. Percentile distributions of the value of food consumption (1840 farm prices)

	1775	1840 Free men and house	1909	1948
	Soldiers	servants	Total population	
Meat, fish, poultry	50	49	27	23
Grains	17	18	10	5
Basic meat and grain diet (lines 1 & 2)	66	67	37	28
Vegetables and fruits	9	12	29	32
Dairy products and eggs	10	16	22	27
Sugar and syrups	15	5	12	13
Total	100	100	100	100

SOURCES: Valuation: In so far as possible, components of diet were converted into their raw constituents (U.S., Production and Marketing Administration, *Conversion Factors and Weights and Measures for Agricultural Commodities and Their Products* [Washington, D.C., May 1952]) and valued by use of the farm prices for 1840 given by Marvin W. Towne and Wayne D. Rasmussen in National Bureau of Economic Research, Conference on Income and Wealth, *Trends in the American Economy in the Nineteenth Century*, Studies in Income and Wealth, XXIV (Princeton, N.J., 1960), 283–305.

Diet schedules: 1775: John Fitzpatrick (ed.) *The Writings of George Washington* (Washington, D.C., 1931), III, 409. The entry is headed, "The following is the Ration of Provisions allowed by the Continental Congress unto each Soldier."

a. *1 lb. of fresh beef or 3/4 lb. of pork or 1 lb. of fish per day*. The calculations in the table assume 1 pound of meat per day, valued at the mean price of beef and pork for 1840. The one-pound-per-day regimen was selected because it commonly appears in the militia records and therefore was probably typical.

b. *1 lb. of bread or flour per day*. I assumed the bread was hardtack (pilot bread). Wheat converts into flour and hardtack at the same rate (U.S., Production and Marketing Administration, 38).

c. *3 pints of peas or beans per week or "vegetables equivalent."* The calculations assume that the ration was typically peas and beans.

d. *1 pint of milk per day "when to be had."* The calculations assume that milk was regularly "to be had."

e. *1/2 pint of rice or 1 pint of Indian meal per week*. The calculations rest on the corn ration. The choice affects the table little.

f. *1 quart of spruce beer per day or 9 gallons of molasses per company of 100 men*. My calculations rest on the molasses ration, since I could find no 1840 price for spruce beer.

1840: Ezra C. Seaman, *Essays on the Progress of Nations* (New York, 1852), diets of free men and house servants, 278, 279 (fish only), 280 (sugar, molasses, rice). I added 50 pounds to the meat component (see text and n. 18; supplementing the Seaman figure by 100 pounds raises the share of meat in the diet to 54 percent; following the Seaman schedule as given reduces the share of meat in the diet to 43 shifts in the structure of population.[22] Consequently, one can form rough estimates of real per capita consumption of perishables at each date before 1840 by adding to the data in Table 2 the estimates of the value of firewood consumption, discussed earlier in this section. The figures appear in Table 4, together with David's estimates of per capita real GDP. The last two columns in the table were derived by subtracting per capita perishables consumption from per capita GDP, and they therefore show the implicit real value of consumption of semidurables, durables and services, as well as the value of

TABLE 4.   Estimates of per capita real GDP and components, 1790–1840 (1840 prices)

	GDP		Fuel con-sump-tion	Nonfuel perish-ables con-sump-tion	Col. 3 & col. 4	Implicit Flow of Nonperishables	
						Variant I	Variant II
	Variant I	Variant II				Col. 1 minus col. 5	Col. 2 minus col. 5
1790	—	$50	$7	$35	$42	—	$ 8
1800	$55	58	7	35	42	$13	16
1810	52	56	7	36	43	9	13
1820	58	61	7	36	43	15	18
1830	74	76	7	37	44	30	32
1840	91	91	7	38	45	46	46

SOURCES: Col. 1 and 2 (Variants I and II of GDP): Table 1.   Col. 3: see text. Col. 4: Table 2.

percent) and assumed that the "rye, corn, buckwheat" component consisted exclusively of corn. I valued the meat ration at $4.50 per hundred pounds (the mean of the Towne and Rasmussen pork and beef prices), following the same procedure for all dates (see n. 12).

1909 and 1948: Ralph W. Gerard, *et al.*, *Food for Life* (Chicago, 1952), 268 (excluding coffee, tea and cocoa). Dairy products include fats and oils. All vegetables and fruits except for potatoes were valued at the Towne and Rasmussen price for peas and beans ($1.19 per bushel, or about $.02 per pound).

[22]I have not mentioned changes across time in the importance of food processing as a source by which the value of food consumption might have risen before 1840. The subject is discussed in a broader context in the next section. For the moment it is enough to say that value added by the manufacture of foods in 1840 came to only about $36 million (Studies in Income and Wealth, XXIV, 59, and XXX, 36, n. c), or less than 5 percent of the value of perishables flowing to consumers (XXX, 27). It is doubtful that this fraction was materially lower in earlier decades.

investment, at each date. The residuals associated with the first four years in the table are very small, indeed unrealistically small. Assuming my estimates of the real value of per capita perishables consumption are accurate, David's per capita GDP estimates for these years must be too low, and therefore, his computed rate of change must be too high. These results cannot be regarded as conclusive since the data on which the estimates before 1840 rest are very flimsy. But they are suggestive and point the way to a more comprehensive test through a thoroughgoing study of dietary standards.

IV

The secure evidence David found at hand when he began to construct his product estimates was limited indeed. But he recognized that he did not need precisely accurate figures for his purposes. His series had to be good enough to test the Rostow "take-off" hypothesis and to pick up long swings. I want to leave aside the question of the long swings altogether and give full attention to the long-term rate of change. Rostow asserts that there was a long-term acceleration of the rate of change dating from the 1840s, a proposition David finds dubious. Consequently, David's estimating procedure had to be designed so as to assure that the pre-1840 product estimates were not biased in a downward direction; i.e., he had to be careful not to overstate the pre-1840 growth rate and thus stack the deck against the Rostow hypothesis. He was well aware of this requirement and made strong efforts to meet it. The preceding section suggests that he may have failed. I now want to take up his estimating procedure with the object of discovering where, if at all, he erred. I will consider only the period from 1800 to 1840. David's extension of the series to 1790 depends upon very chancy data and is not nearly so strong as the work for the subsequent period.

David has six sets of data he is willing to accept and one fundamental assumption he believes is sound. The first five sets of data consist of estimates at decade intervals, 1800–1840, of the following: (1) population; (2) total labor force; (3) agricultural labor force; (4) nonagricultural labor force; and (5) agricultural output, expressed in prices of 1840. The sixth set refers to 1840 and consists of estimates of: (6) output per worker in each of the two sectors, agriculture and nonagriculture. The fundamental assumption is that: (7) nonagricultural labor productivity (output divided by labor force) grew at least as fast as agricultural labor productivity over the period 1800–1840.

Notice what he can do with this information. From items 3 and 5 he can compute agricultural output per worker at each relevant date. With this series in hand and the information contained in items 6 and 7 he can compute the maximum level of output per nonagricultural worker at each date. (Since he knows the level of nonagricultural output per worker in 1840, item 6, and the lowest rate at which it could have grown in earlier decades, item 7 plus the series on agricultural productivity, he can compute the highest level it could have reached at each date before 1840.) With these data and the series described in item 4 he can calculate the maximum level of total nonagricultural output at each date. The sum of nonagricultural output and agricultural output, item 5, is real gross domestic product. Dividing item 1 by real GDP yields product per capita. David can now calculate the rate of growth. More precisely, he can calculate the lowest rate at which growth could have taken place, if his data are accurate and his fundamental assumption is sound. His results show that the pace of growth was not substantially slower before 1840 than afterward.

I now want to take up each piece of evidence and each step in the procedure. Since the population series almost certainly introduces no bias into David's results, I will put it aside and begin with the labor force estimates.

The underlying labor force figures were produced, with great care and skill, by Stanley Lebergott.[23] It is impossible to do this work justice in the limited space I have, and I must therefore leave the basic data and procedures unexplored. It is clear, however, that Lebergott's estimates, especially those relating to the earlier years in the period, are accurate only within fairly wide limits, a point Lebergott himself would surely accept. In fact, David corrects several of the estimates, in the case of the 1800 figures adjusting the total downward by almost 12 percent and markedly altering the distribution of the total between the agricultural and nonagricultural components. That the changes are important can be readily seen. If one reestimates per capita GDP in 1800, following David's procedure but using Leber-

[23]Studies in Income and Wealth, XXX, 116-20.

gott's original labor force estimates, the result obtained is 20 percent above the per capita GDP value estimated by David. More to the point, David's estimate of the advance in per capita GDP (Variant II) between 1800 and 1840 is 56 percent. Substituting the 1800 figure based on Lebergott's work would lower the result to roughly 30 percent and would alter David's fundamental conclusion.

Now it may very well be that David's decision to change Lebergott's work was correct. Certainly it appears that Lebergott failed to follow his procedures consistently and that he may have obtained a larger total value for 1800 than his methods dictate. Nonetheless, one experiences feelings of unease about the sensitivity of David's results to the changes he has made in the labor force figures, particularly as the changes affect the distribution of the total between sectors, an important matter for the GDP estimates. A crucial element in David's defense of his results is his judgment of what constitutes a plausible value for the ratio of free rural male nonagricultural secondary workers to free rural nonagricultural households.[24] David appraises the plausibility of the value he selects in terms of the magnitude of the ratio of all secondary workers to all household heads. But at a time when most free rural households were headed by farmers and farm workers, rural nonagricultural secondary workers were probably supplied in important numbers by agricultural households, and thus the ratio of all free male rural nonagricultural secondary workers to nonagricultural rural households could plausibly assume a very large value. The aggregate ratio—all secondary workers to all households—provides no secure guide, and in the absence of other evidence we have no way of choosing between the ratios offered by Lebergott and David. We cannot be sure that David's estimates are not biased in favor of his hypothesis.

David offers two estimates of the 1840 ratio of agricultural to nonagricultural productivity (item 6). He interprets the two within the same conventional conceptual framework. But the data from which one of the two was computed were drawn from an unconventional measurement.[25] It seems to me that a good case can be made for the explicit acceptance of the unconventional measure, a matter I want to take up in more detail subsequently. The only points that

[24]See David, "Memorandum 53A."

[25]See Stanley Engerman's discussion of David's paper in the *American Economic Review*, LVII (May 1967), 308, 309.

need be made here are that the unconventional measure yields the higher values in the ranges of figures contained in Table 1, and, of course, they describe a lower rate of change than do the figures based on the conventional measure.

The last series in the list measures agricultural output at decade intervals, 1800–1840. It rests on the work of Marvin W. Towne and Wayne D. Rasmussen, which consists chiefly of extrapolations from subsequent experience.[26] In effect, Towne and Rasmussen have assumed what must be proved, for David's purposes. David attempts to show that the rates of change of agricultural productivity implicit in the agricultural labor force and output series are reasonable. But the proofs are not compelling, and Stanley Engerman has persuasively argued that the implied rate of change for the 1830s, at least, is probably too high, a result which is unfavorable to David's case since it suggests a bias in his computed rate of growth that favors his hypothesis.[27] Nonetheless, I am not at all sure that the productivity test fails because of errors in the output series. The labor force estimates may well be at fault. In the previous section of this lecture I have suggested that per capita consumption of food may have increased little from decade to decade over the period 1800–1840. If I am right, then farm production of foods must have increased at about the same rate as population, since most food production was for domestic consumption and most domestic consumption of food came out of domestic production. This is precisely the assumption underlying the Towne and Rasmussen estimates of food output.

There is another aspect of the output series that troubles me, however. David's procedure involves the implicit assumption that the output of agricultural workers consisted solely of agricultural products. But of course agricultural workers also produced investments in farm lands (clearing, fencing and so on) and engaged in home manufacturing. There is evidence that at least the latter kind of activities was relatively more important before 1840 than afterward.[28] Therefore, there is reason to suppose that David's esti-

[26]Studies in Income and Wealth, XXIV, 255-317. For the years 1840 onward, the Towne and Rasmussen series rest quite firmly on output and inventory data. But see the comments in n. 18.

[27]Engerman, 308.

[28]See Rolla M. Tryon, *Household Manufactures in the United States, 1640-1860* (Chicago, 1917), passim.

mates of agricultural productivity are biased downward and that the problem grows progressively more serious as his series extends backward in time.

We have here an example of what Simon Kuznets has called the problem of conceptual scope.[29] The conventional domestic product estimates omit the proceeds of several types of activity conducted beyond the confines of the market. If these activities change in relative importance across time, the conventional measures give a biased account of growth. Typically, of course, the bias is in an upward direction, since the process of growth tends to bring more and more economic activities into the market. For example, the conventional measures yield an average rate of growth (real per capita GNP) of about 16 percent per decade for the years 1840–1900, while an unconventional measure, which takes into account investment in land clearing and home manufacturing, gives a rate of only 13 percent.[30]

David recognizes the problem and points out that his omission of land clearing and home manufacturing is intentional. He believes that a proper test of the Rostow hypothesis involves the use of conventional measures, with the focus on market-bound activities. But this defense is not adequate. The conventional measures include the proceeds of important activities that are not directed toward markets. Examples are food produced by farmers for their own consumption and the imputed rental value of owner-occupied houses. Many of the non-market-bound activities excluded from the conventional measures are excluded simply because they are no longer very important. The decision in these cases rests on no theoretical consideration, and therefore, David cannot properly determine the product concept he will use by appeal to modern practice. However, it is important to notice that David's case against Rostow might be strengthened were he to use the unconventional measure I have proposed. My guess is that it would yield an acceleration across a very extended period of time and would tell against the notion of an abrupt transition from low to high rates of change.

[29]Kuznets, "Quantitative Aspects of the Economic Growth of Nations, I. Levels and Variability of Rates of Growth," *Economic Development and Cultural Change*, V (Oct. 1956), 6.

[30]See Studies in Income and Wealth, XXX, 9, Table 2, for average rates of change of real GNP per capita, Variants I and II, over the decades bounded by 1834–43 and 1894–1903.

We come finally to David's fundamental assumption that labor productivity grew faster in nonagriculture than in agriculture over the
period 1800–1840. David supports this position by reference to experience in manufacturing, where productivity may have been growing rapidly before 1840. But at the end of the period in question, income earned in manufacturing could not have accounted for much
more than one-quarter of total nonagricultural income, and the
share must have been smaller in earlier years.[31] Productivity growth
in nonagriculture before 1840 must have been dominated by experience in nonmanufacturing activities, specifically, by experience in
construction and the services. There is no reason to suppose that productivity in these activities grew as fast as productivity in agriculture.
Furthermore, an important shift in the structure of nonagricultural
output almost certainly tended to reduce the level of labor productivity in the sector. An important component of nonagricultural output
throughout this period was the shelter value of dwellings. Now this
service is produced by capital; labor's direct role is negligible. Other
things being equal, an increase in the share of nonagricultural output
accounted for by this service would tend to raise the computed productivity of nonagricultural labor, and vice versa. This is so because
changes in the output of this service alter the numerator of the
productivity ratio (output) without materially affecting the denominator (labor). It is virtually a certainty that the share of nonagricultural output accounted for by the service of shelter fell in the decades before 1840, exerting a downward pressure on labor productivity.

Finally there is, once more, the problem of domestic production.
David's measures of productivity advance in manufacturing relate
to the factory-mill-shop component of the sector. But nonagricultural
households also produced goods at home. The measured advance of
manufacturing productivity—output divided by workers attached to
factories, mills and shops—would be very much smaller were proper
account taken of home production by nonfarm households.

Perhaps the point can be clarified if I approach it from another direction. Between 1800 and 1840, American factory production of
manufactured goods grew very rapidly and largely displaced home

[31]According to David, "Growth of Real Product," 168, nonfarm gross product in
1840 ran between $906 and $936 million. Value added by manufacturing was only
$250 million in that year (Studies in Income and Wealth, XXIV, 59, and XXX, 47, n.
e), and gross income originating was less than this.

production.[32] Now David's estimates of the labor force, the distribution of the labor force between sectors and levels of productivity in the two sectors ignore this phenomenon. It seems likely to me that the number of persons engaged in important production in, for example, 1800 was larger than the number David allocates to the work force. Women and children were more heavily engaged than David supposes. Furthermore, occupational lines were less clearcut in 1800 than in 1840 or in 1860. A farmer, his wife and his sons and daughters might spend most of the spring, summer and early fall in agricultural pursuits. But the rest of the year they were chiefly engaged in manufacturing and the production of services, such as blacksmithing or transportation. Estimates of output that depend on patterns of behavior at subsequent dates are bound to result in an underestimate of production in 1800. Of course the problem is not confined to the pre-1840 period, but there is good reason to suppose that it is far more serious in these decades than subsequently.[33]

V

What conclusions can one draw from the thoughts gathered in the preceding four sections? First, it seems to me that the topic David has taken up is an exceptionally important one. The pace and character of economic change in the first five or six decades of the new republic have been the subject of wide and inconclusive debate. David is entirely correct in supposing that the issues involved are largely quantitative and aggregative in nature and that they can be satisfactorily resolved only if we are able to assemble acceptable measures of total product. His approach to the problem is admirably simple and lucid, and I think that his results, in the manner of Kuznets's classic essay,[34] are strong enough to support the proposition that the econ-

[32]Tryon, especially the last chapter.

[33]*Ibid.* See also, the exchange between Solomon Fabricant, on the one hand, and T. J. Weiss and R. E. Gallman, on the other, published in National Bureau of Economic Research, Conference on Research in Income and Wealth, *Conference on the Size Distribution of Income and Wealth*, Studies in Income and Wealth, XXXIII (New York, 1969), 368–71, 379–81.

[34]Simon Kuznets, "Long-Term Changes in the National Income of the United States of America since 1870," and appendix, "Current National Income Estimates for the Period Prior to 1870," in Kuznets (ed.), *Income and Wealth of the United States, Trends and Structure* (Cambridge, Eng., 1952), 221-41.

omy was not stagnant before 1840, that growth was indeed taking place. In the sections of the papers that I have not discussed he has also made a good case for the long-swing hypothesis.

At the same time I must say that I doubt that growth was proceeding as rapidly as David supposes, and I doubt that there was no long-term acceleration in the pace of change. I do not mean that Rostow's conception of a rather abrupt acceleration dated to the 1840s is correct. The change may have been very gradual, indeed, and the high rates recorded from the mid-1840s to the mid-1850s may very well reflect a long swing, rather than a fundamental shift of the kind Rostow describes. But we cannot choose between these two interpretations with confidence until we have a clearer conception of the level of product early in the century. It seems to me that we require measures based on a broader concept than the one used by David—measures that take into account more of the productive activity organized in the home. Despite these reservations, it seems clear to me that David's substantive contribution is important. Furthermore, he has written two essays of rare grace, frankness and clarity.

VII The Statistical Approach
The Input-Output System

Dorothy S. Brady

THE TRANSACTIONS MATRIX

THE input-output system is a theoretical scheme worked out by Wassily W. Leontief for the analysis of interindustry relations.[1] This scheme depends on a statistical description of the flow of products passing from one industry to another or going to final demand. The statistical description which is known as the input-output table or the transactions matrix is a cross classification in which each industry is represented by a row and a column; final demand appears in bordering columns on the right and payments to primary factors are shown in bordering rows at the bottom (see Table 1). The rows of the table show where the output went. The columns of the table detail the inputs in the form of materials and services coming from other industries and of the services of primary factors such as capital and labor. The total across each row for the industrial sector is equal to the total for the corresponding column since, by definition, total gross input equals total gross output.

The distinction between the production of goods and services and their final disposition is exhibited by the division of the table into four quadrants as outlined in Table 1. The top left quadrant, I, shows interindustry transactions, the production and disposition of intermediate goods and services. The top right quadrant, II, records the transactions involved in meeting final demand, specified by sector, from the output of domestic industries. The bottom quadrant on the left, III, shows the payment by industries for primary factors, which include imports for use in industry. The bottom quadrant on the right, IV, shows the payments by the sectors of final demand for primary inputs. The definition of these sectors and their placement in the table often vary, and frequently the fourth quadrant is omitted.

[1]Leontief, *The Structure of the American Economy, 1919–1939*, 2nd ed. (New York, 1951).

TABLE 1.   The transactions matrix.

	Producing sectors	Final demand	Total output
Producing sectors	I. Intermediate production and consumption	II. Final output of producing sectors	
Primary factors	III. Primary inputs to production	IV. Primary inputs to final demand	
Total input			

It is the first quadrant that makes the transaction matrix much more comprehensive than the national accounting aggregates which can be derived from the other three quadrants. The intermediate production and consumption is given in the detail determined by the number of industrial sectors, with the result that the first quadrant takes by far the greatest space in the table. If thirty industries were distinguished, each with a row and a column, the grid would contain 900 cells.

THE INDUSTRIAL CLASSIFICATION

As with all statistical systems, the empirical work going into the construction of the transactions matrix necessarily involves a compromise between theoretical considerations and feasibility. Feasibility is determined by the nature of the sources of data, both actual and potential, and the cost, in time and money, of preparing the table. A very detailed classification of industries might well be easier to construct if the basic data were available and cost was no consideration. With a very small number of industrial sectors, the table would lose its intrinsic meaning as a description of the interdependence in the industrial structure. Some theoretical concepts have to guide the classification toward a level that provides empirically meaningful results.

The concept that has been used for this purpose is known as the homogeneity assumption. Homogeneity in the input structure is desirable because considerable variability in the process of production within sectors would blur the differences between sectors, which are of primary interest for purposes of description and interpretation. Homogeneity in the output structure is desirable because there should be no ambiguities in the allocation of final products to the various industries. Classification into a small number of sectors implies considerable variability in the composition of inputs for the varied collection of goods and services included in the output of each sector. Classification in great detail implies that the output of a particular sector is not unique in its final use or, in other words, that the goods and services produced in various sectors could be and often are substitutes in final demand. These considerations have lead in practice to classifications that distinguish a modest number of sectors compared to the thousands of goods and services that flow to final consumers.

A table with 450 sectors such as the one constructed by the Bureau of Labor Statistics for the United States in 1947[2] is large in comparison with those compiled for most other countries. Most tables, including the most current for the United States, relating to 1958, distinguish fewer than 100 industrial sectors. Although detailed classifications will continue to interest the economists engaged in analyzing the structure of the current economy, it is likely that, as attention is focused on historical and international or interregional comparisons, comparability will become an increasingly important desideratum in the definition of the industrial sectors. Prior to 1958 intertemporal comparisons had been made only for the United States, Denmark and Norway, and these comparisons were made to check the degree of stability in the input structure over relatively short periods of time. In 1958 Hollis B. Chenery and Tsunehiko Watanabe published the results of an international comparison covering four countries, the United States, Japan, Norway and Italy.[3] To carry out the comparison, the authors had to reduce the tables for each country to a smaller number of sectors which were the same for all four countries. The extension of the comparison to many more countries would be difficult, if not impossible, because of differences in the conventions used in the compilation of the tables.

Historians are always concerned with comparability in definitions

---

[2]W. Duane Evans and Marvin Hoffenberg, "The Interindustry relations study for 1947," *Review of Economics and Statistics*, XXXIV (May 1952), 97–142.

[3]Chenery and Watanabe, "International Comparisons of the Structure of Production," *Econometrica*, XXVI (July 1958), 487–521.

and concepts, but in principle there is no difference between comparisons over time and comparisons over space. Unless the classification is the same, comparisons are impossible. True, the particular sector in two or more situations may differ greatly in its composition, but if it represents the same end use, then comparisons can be meaningful and can lead to the discovery of new explanations for historical changes or international and interregional differences. William G. Whitney's use of the twenty-nine sectors defined by Chenery and Watanabe is significant, for it will, no doubt, set the pattern for the construction of other tables for the nineteenth century.[4]

THE SOURCES OF DATA

Once the industrial classification is determined, the frame of the input-output table is specified. The headings in the first quadrant are the specified industries for both the columns and the rows. This square arrangement is the interindustry matrix. The headings for the second quadrant are the specified industries for the rows and the sectors of final demand for the columns. The sectors of final demand that are commonly distinguished are households, governments, exports, gross private capital formation and net increase in inventories. The headings for the third quadrant are the primary factors for the rows and the specified industries for the columns. The primary factors include imports, payments to government and depreciation allowances as well as employees' income and profits. The headings for the fourth quadrant are the primary factors and the sectors of final demand. The summary column for the entire table is total output and the summary row is total input, which for the industries in the rows and corresponding columns are the same.

The estimation of the magnitudes for each cell in the table generally proceeds from the bordering totals for the whole table to bordering subtotals for the first quadrant, the interindustry matrix. Industrial censuses provide the source data on the total output in manufacturing, agriculture, mining and power generation. Censuses, surveys and reports of agencies such as the Interstate Commerce Commission are

[4]Whitney, "The Structure of the American Economy in the Late Nineteenth Century," Discussion Paper Number 80, Department of Economics, University of Pennsylvania, mimeographed (1968).

the basic sources for transportation, fuel and energy. Where such sources exist, the estimation of the totals for the transactions matrix is largely a matter of aggregation from quite detailed classifications to the level specified for the table. For other industries, particularly trade and some of the services, the output figures may have to be derived from the occupational censuses and information on the average incomes of the primary factors andoon the other inputs to production. Statistics produced by the supervisory authorities and later the Federal Deposit Insurance Corporation have provided the basic data on banking services, while the commercial publications and trade associations have provided the basic data on life insurance. These are some of the same source materials as are used in the construction of national accounts. The preparation of input-output tables generally benefits from the considerable work with source data already summarized for purposes of estimating the national product and expenditure.

The summary row of the interindustry table is generally derived by subtracting payments to primary factors from total output. The distribution of the total intermediate input to the separate industries depends on information that is gleaned from many sources. Special censuses and surveys, reports of regulatory agencies, commercial publications, engineering handbooks and studies of particular industries are some of the source materials consulted. In the preparation of tables for the recent past, surveys and experts' opinions have been used to supplement the information available in such sources. In the construction of tables for the distant past, the compiler is completely dependent on the data on the costs of operation that can be located in the diverse sources used by historians. Compiling a table for the 1840s, for example, would depend for its success on finding information in such sources as the business press and other publications dealing with economic matters, in handbooks of various kinds and in business histories.

The summary column of the interindustry table is derived by subtracting the national accounting aggregates for final demand, appropriately adjusted, from total output. The work sheet for Table 2 shows the totals for the rows and columns that are the controls for the estimates of the cell values. Distribution of the column totals on the basis of information on costs will yield numbers for the cells of the table that in all likelihood will not add across the rows to the con-

TABLE 2.   The interindustry transactions table.

Sales by specified sector, rows	Purchases by specified sector, columns							Total
	A	B	C	–	–	–	–	
A								
B								
C								
–								
–								
–								
Total								

trol totals in the summary column. The reconciliation in this situation cannot be described apart from a knowledge of the nature of the particular sources used in the compilation of the estimates. This is one of the reasons for the length of time required for the construction of the input-output table; good practice in statistical work rules out arbitrary adjustment of estimates to the greatest possible extent and requires adjustments in accordance with some kind of objective evidence.

If information on the sales of each industry to other industries could be amassed, a second set of estimates for the cells of the interindustry table could be determined, and with two sets of estimates reconciliation becomes much more difficult. Sales to different industrial classes of users are less commonly available in the sources of data than purchases from various classes of industries, although information on which to base the distribution of sales across the rows might be collected in special surveys or censuses. Thus generally it is from the cost data that the cell values are determined.

In the construction of input-output tables for historical periods the compiler depends, to a very great extent, on prior research carried out in conjunction with the estimation of national accounting aggregates or for other purposes. Industry studies such as are found in Volumes XXIV and XXX of Studies in Income and Wealth were designed to make a contribution to the national accounts.[5] The needs

[5]National Bureau of Economic Research, Conference on Research in Income and Wealth, *Trends in the American Economy in the Nineteenth Century*, Studies in Income and Wealth, XXIV (Princeton, N.J., 1960), and *Output, Employment and Productivity in the United States after 1800*, Studies in Income and Wealth, XXX (New York, 1966).

for national or regional accounting are likely to affect a wide range of research in the future. It is quite possible that, in addition to industrial histories, business histories and regional studies, some research in the history of technology will be affected by the possibilities of contributions to the compilation of input-output tables.

Comparability over time and between nations or regions has led to some measure of uniformity in definitions and concepts, matters which are given much space in the literature on the empirical work connected with the compilation of the transactions matrix. Transactions are, preferably, valued in producer's prices. When they are, marketing costs are shown as inputs from the appropriate sector, such as transport, trade, financial services or government, to the producing industry.

Output is preferably gross of intraindustry transactions because in reducing the table to a smaller number of sectors through aggregation for comparative studies, the total sum of all transactions remains the same; whereas when output is taken net of intraindustry transactions the total changes in the process of aggregation.

There are various schemes for the treatment of secondary products that do not share the same input structure. Allocation is made where possible to the industry for which the joint product or the by-product is the principal form of its output. If there is no such industry, an artificial sector may be created for the accounting balance. Such works as the bulletins of international agencies on input-output analysis give considerable attention to the problems involved in the allocations.[6]

Data on sales and purchases have to be adjusted for changes in inventories. The changes may be recorded, gross, the increases as a sector of final demand and the decreases as a sector in payments to primary factors. Alternatively they may appear, net, as a sector of final demand.

Exports are generally shown as a sector of final demand. Imports are treated in various ways, as a row in quadrants III and IV of Table 1 or as an addition to the domestic production of similar goods and services. If they are so added, their total is shown in final demand as a sum to be taken negatively. A combination of placing noncompeting imports in a row among the primary factors and allocating competing

[6]United Nations Statistical Office, *Problems of Input-Output Tables and Analysis* (New York, 1965).

imports to the industries producing similar products is frequently used.

Direct taxes are not generally entered in the tables, whereas indirect taxes are generally entered among the rows for primary inputs. Sales taxes will appear at the intersection of the indirect taxes row and the domestic consumption column.

The adjustments in the original data to conform to such definitions are numerous indeed, and the working papers for an interindustry study fill very large manuals.

COEFFICIENTS OF DIRECT AND INDIRECT REQUIREMENTS PER UNIT OF FINAL DEMAND

From the information in the transactions table it is possible to calculate the additional units of input that would be required to provide for an expansion in final demand for the products of one or more industries. To carry out the calculations, a table of input coefficients is derived from the interindustry part of the transactions table, and the coefficients are used in equations that show how the output of each sector depends on the final demand for the products of every sector. To illustrate how the equations are derived, the numbers in the transactions table are replaced by symbols in Table 3. The x's are inputs,

TABLE 3. The transactions table in symbols.

Sales by specified sector, rows	Purchases by specified sector, columns			Final demand	Total
	1	2	3		
1	x_{11}	x_{12}	x_{13}	Y_1	X_1
2	x_{21}	x_{22}	x_{23}	Y_2	X_2
3	x_{31}	x_{32}	x_{33}	Y_3	X_3
Primary factors	V_1	V_2	V_3	V_4	V
Total	X_1	X_2	X_3	Y	T

with the first subscript representing the row and the second subscript the column. The X's are outputs, with the subscript designating the industrial sector. The Y's are the final demand for product of the industry shown by the subscript, and the V's are the payments to primary factors or value added. The fact that the sums across the rows equal total outputs for the industrial sectors can then be expressed in a set of three equations:

(Set 1)
$$x_{11} + x_{12} + x_{13} + Y_1 = X_1$$

$$x_{21} + x_{22} + x_{23} + Y_2 = X_2$$

$$x_{31} + x_{32} + x_{33} + Y_3 = X_3$$

This set of equations simply reproduces the information shown in Table 3.

TABLE 4.   Direct purchases per dollar of output.

Sales by specified sector, rows	Purchases by specified sector		
	1	2	3
1	a_{11}	a_{12}	a_{13}
2	a_{21}	a_{22}	a_{23}
3	a_{31}	a_{32}	a_{33}
Primary factors	b_1	b_2	b_3
Total	1	1	1

Dividing the inputs in each column of the transactions table yields the table of direct requirements, called the input coefficients—(Table 4). The a's and b's are symbols for the input coefficients, which express each input as a ratio to total output. If all the coefficients were multiplied by 100, each column in the table would show the percentage distribution of the inputs in each specific industry.

The table of input coefficients specifies the direct requirements for the production of one unit of output by each industry. Thus in producing 1,000 dollars of its output, industry spends 1,000 times a_{21} dollars for the product of industry 2. To produce these goods and services industry 2 purchases inputs, and such inputs call for further inputs. The successions of inputs required to produce the goods and services purchased by each industry are called the indirect requirements. Total requirements can be determined by an algebraic procedure, and the subtraction of the direct requirements from the totals yields the sums of the indirect requirements.

Multiplying the coefficients by the total output reproduces the original table (Table 3) because the coefficients were calculated through division by total output for each column. The symbolic scheme in Table 5 expresses the relations in the transactions table in a form that

TABLE 5.   The transactions table showing the input coefficients.

Sales by specified sector	Purchases by specified sector			Final demand	Total
	1	2	3		
1	$a_{11}X_1$	$a_{12}X_2$	$a_{13}X_3$	Y_1	X_1
2	$a_{21}X_1$	$a_{22}X_2$	$a_{23}X_3$	Y_2	X_2
3	$a_{31}X_1$	$a_{32}X_2$	$a_{33}X_3$	Y_3	X_3
Primary factors	b_1X_1	b_2X_2	b_3X_3		
Total	X_1	X_2	X_3		

can be used to show how total output in each industry is related to the final demand for the output of every industry.

The fact that the sum of each row in Table 5 equals the total output can be expressed in three equations for the industrial sectors:

(Set 2)
$$a_{11}X_1 + a_{12}X_2 + a_{13}X_3 + Y_1 = X_1$$

$$a_{21}X_1 + a_{22}X_2 + a_{23}X_3 + Y_2 = X_2$$

$$a_{31}X_1 + a_{32}X_2 + a_{33}X_3 + Y_3 = X_3$$

The equations in Set 2 representing the row sums are then recast to show the final demand terms Y_1, Y_2, and Y_3 on the right-hand side:

(Set 3)
$$X_1 - a_{11}X_1 - a_{12}X_2 - a_{13}X_3 = Y_1$$

$$X_2 - a_{21}X_1 + -a_{22}X_2 - a_{23}X_3 = Y_2$$

$$X_3 - a_{31}X_1 - a_{32}X_2 + -a_{33}X_3 = Y_3$$

This set of equations simply states that total output in each industry, the X's, minus the intermediate demand from every industry, equals final demand. Combining the terms in X_1, X_2, and X_3 in the sequence of equations makes the coefficients in the diagonal terms read: $1 - a_{11}$, $1 - a_{22}$, $1 - a_{33}$.

Taking the input coefficients, the a's, and final demand, the Y's, as given and the output levels as unknowns, the equations can be solved to show how output levels depend on final demand directly and indirectly. The algebraic solution of this set of simultaneous equations is another set of equations in which the coefficients represent the total direct and indirect requirements per unit of final demand:

(Set 4)
$$A_{11} Y_1 + A_{12} Y_2 + A_{13} Y_3 = X_1$$

$$A_{21} Y_1 + A_{22} Y_2 + A_{23} Y_3 = X_2$$

$$A_{31} Y_1 + A_{32} Y_2 + A_{33} Y_3 = X_3$$

The equations in Set 4 tell how to calculate the direct and indirect requirements for the output of each industry, the X's, given the Y's, and a table of the total requirements per unit of final demand (Table 6).

TABLE 6. Direct and indirect requirements per dollar of final demand.

| Sector | Final demand for output from specified sector | | |
	1	2	3
1	A_{11}	A_{12}	A_{13}
2	A_{21}	A_{22}	A_{23}
3	A_{31}	A_{32}	A_{33}

Acquaintance with the algebra underlying their derivation is not needed to understand the meaning of these coefficients. The term A_{12} is the total requirement for the output of the first industry per unit of final demand and for the output of the second industry. The meaning of the other coefficients is similar.

With a table of the total requirements per unit of final demand (Table 6) and the input coefficient table, (Table 4), the direct and indirect requirements corresponding to specified levels of demand can be calculated. To produce 1,000 units for the final demand for the products of every industry the coefficients in the equations in Set 4 are all multiplied by 1,000 and then summed. The resulting sums are the total output levels required. Subtracting 1,000 plus the direct requirements calculated from the input coefficient table (Table 4) gives the magnitudes of the indirect requirements.

On the assumption that the input coefficients are quite stable, the equations relating output levels to final demand have become an important tool for forecasting, planning and decision-making. There is no other technique for estimating all the direct and indirect requirements for sustaining a given level of final demand.

The number of problems for which the equations in Set 4 provide quantitative solutions depend on the number of sectors that are distinguished in final demand. Generally domestic consumption, capital formation and exports are given separately, and frequently competitive imports are shown as a negative category. The equations in Set 4 can be applied directly to any sector of final demand such as exports or imports. Thus the negative effect on domestic industries of increasing imports can be estimated by substituting the new levels of imports for the Y's and multiplying the new levels of the Y's by the coefficients as indicated.

DIRECT AND INDIRECT EFFECTS
CONNECTED WITH THE PRICES OF PRIMARY FACTORS

The fact that totals for the columns in Tables 3 and 5 add to the total output can also be expressed as a set of equations, but as Table 3 shows, the division of every input by the same number leaves all the equations with unity on the right-hand side. These equations, corresponding to those in Set 2, make up Set 5:

(Set 5)
$$a_{11} + a_{21} + a_{31} + b_1 = 1$$

$$a_{12} + a_{22} + a_{32} + b_2 = 1$$

$$a_{13} + a_{23} + a_{33} + b_3 = 1$$

To use these equations to show how the prices of primary factors are related to other prices in the economic system the coefficients must be construed as quantity ratios. When the physical unit is defined as the quantity that can be sold for one dollar, the quantity ratios are the same as the value ratios. If the coefficients were based on the actual physical units, they would no longer be additive. To make them additive, each coefficient must be multiplied by the ratio of the input price to the output price.

Since the price of the output is a common denominator in each transformed equation, it can be transferred to the right-hand side. The result is a system of equations relating the prices of the inputs, including the primary factors, to the prices of the outputs:

(Set 6)
$$a_{11}p_1 + a_{21}p_2 + a_{31}p_3 + b_1r_1 = p_1$$

$$a_{12}p_1 + a_{22}p_2 + a_{32}p_3 + b_2r_2 = p_2$$

$$a_{13}p_1 + a_{23}p_2 + a_{33}p_3 + b_3r_3 = p_3$$

Here p_1, p_2, p_3 are the prices for the output of the three industries and r_1, r_2 and r_3 are the "prices" of the primary factors. These equations can be solved for p_1, p_2 and p_3 just as those in Set 2 were solved for the outputs X_1, X_2 and X_3. The result, Set 7, resembles Set 4:

(Set 7)
$$A_{11}b_1r_1 + A_{21}b_2r_2 + A_{31}b_3r_3 = p_1$$

$$A_{12}b_1r_1 + A_{22}b_2r_2 + A_{32}b_3r_3 = p_2$$

$$A_{13}b_1r_1 + A_{23}b_2r_2 + A_{33}b_3r_3 = p_3$$

The A's are the same coefficients as in Set 4, but they are rearranged by displaying them in a table for total requirements (Table 6). In Set 4 the coefficients are read from the rows, whereas in Set 7 the coefficients for the successive equations are read from the columns.

In Set 7, the b's are the known coefficients for total payments to primary factors per unit of output and the r's are composites of the prices for these payments. The b's are sums of input coefficients for the separate factors, such as labor or imports, and consequently the expressions of the form br can be replaced by the sums of the factor input coefficients multiplied by their prices. Suppose the effect of increases in the prices of noncompetitive imports were to be estimated.

In the equations in Set 7 the b's and the r's are replaced by the input coefficients for imports and the ratios of the new prices to the old. An increase of 10 percent in the prices of goods imported by industry 2 would increase the price in industry 1 by 10 percent of A_{21} multiplied by the import coefficient.

With the transactions matrix and the two derived tables, the input coefficient table and the table showing the coefficients for total requirements per unit of final demand, the uses of the system are limited only by the number of sectors into which final demand and factor payments are classified. Often the problem requires the preparation of estimates not provided in the original compilation. To estimate the effect of wage increases in certain industries, with the equations in Set 7, it would be necessary to find out what part of the payrolls could be called wages, apart from salaries. Then the calculations could be made exactly as in the case of imports described above.

The equations showing how prices are related to the unit costs of primary factors (Set 7) give one of the applications that make input-output analysis so popular in planned economies.

TECHNOLOGICAL CHANGE

The connections between industries shown in an interindustry matrix reflect the technical relationships that were current at the given time and place. In the uses described above, the physical inputs per unit of output were assumed to remain stable in the short run. Over the long run only a number of tables spaced to give a description of historical trends will satisfy the economic historian and the analyst of the current economy. In Leontief's words, perhaps the most important task of empirical research is "an intensive and relentless study of structural changes."[7] A voluminous literature of theoretical and empirical studies on the input-output system has accumulated over the past two decades since it became popular. Over the same period studies of productivity and technical change multiplied as technology and related factors such as the skills of the labor force were recognized as explanations of changes or differences in the inputs required to produce a given level of output.

[7] P. 218.

These studies were not based on the unique first quadrant in the transactions matrix; instead they relied on the other quadrants and the marginal totals for the interindustry table. That is, the data used were derived from the national accounts supplemented when necessary by information from other standard statistical sources. The important contributions in this area of research are illustrated in William Whitney's work, where he applies an index number procedure to derive a measure representing technical change in the aggregate.

The concepts of macroeconomics are vast abstractions giving seeming reality to their empirical correlates. Many of the economic magnitudes that are widely used are artificial for they presuppose conditions that did not and probably could not have existed. The gross national product in current dollars is real, but it is the gross national product in constant dollars that is taken for the measure of economic growth. Personal consumption expenditures in current dollars is a real aggregate, but its factoring into a price and a quantity index involves standardizing which is artificial. This is also true of an index derived for technological change in the aggregate.

The index number problem can never be avoided since prices, which are expressed in monetary units, differ between nations, between regions and over time. Furthermore, most of the accounting aggregates including input-output tables are given in values. Direct comparisons of accounts, in current prices, are not generally meaningful because the monetary unit of measurement differs or has changed. Every productivity study is sensitive to the procedure used in converting the estimates to a common unit, the value of the monetary unit in a base situation. The indexes that are calculated, including those derived for technical change, will differ accordingly as price ratios, quantity ratios and other ratios are combined with weights representing a fixed situation, a given year, a given country or a given region.

The comparisons of input coefficient tables, like Table 4, for different years are certain to have an influence on studies of the relation of technological change to productivity and economic growth. In their international comparisons Chenery and Watanabe avoided conversion of the source material to a common monetary unit. But they encountered the index number problem in connection with the summary ratios they defined to measure similarity or dissimilarity in inputs. They made their comparisons of the four countries two at a time. Their indexes weighted the input coefficients of one country with the shares each industry had in the grand total of transactions in the other country. Since the result depended on which of the two countries was taken as a base, they resorted to an index in which the sum of the differences of the coefficients in the corresponding cells of the tables for the two countries, taken without regard to plus or minus sign, was divided by the average of the coefficients.

To lessen the index number problem the average has often been selected for the base situation in comparative studies, but the more distant the time periods, the more difficult the specification for the calculation of the different component averages becomes. It is most likely that the comparisons of input-output tables will follow the practices in national income accounting in the derivations of constant dollar aggregates. This means that the inputs and the outputs are first "deflated" by appropriate price indexes so that the analysis can proceed on the fiction of constant prices through or over all situations covered in the study. When, as is general, the input-output tables are expressed in producers' prices, the appropriate deflators are the wholesale price indexes. Such indexes have been collected by the Bureau of Labor Statistics since 1890. They were compiled by the Aldrich Committee for the years 1860 to 1891 and were assembled by the price historians for earlier years. The Bureau of Labor Statistics is now publishing interindustry sector price indexes for the industries producing commodities included in the wholesale price indexes.[8]

In addition to the basic index number problem, there are many questions connected with deflating to obtain estimates in constant dollars, but these questions are common in all national accounts where constant prices are used. The most unusual problem is one that input-output tables share with the distribution of gross national product by industrial origin. The total payments of primary factors, or value added, is usually deflated by subtracting the deflated inputs purchased from other industries from deflated outputs. This procedure, known as double deflation, can lead and actually has led to negative numbers for value added in constant dollars. Various reasons have been brought forth for such seemingly anomalous results, among them the fact that a residual inherits all the errors in the estimates from which it was

---

[8]U.S., Bureau of Labor Statistics, *Handbook of Labor Statistics, 1967* (Washington, D.C., 1967).

derived. The larger the share of the material inputs in the total output, the larger will be the element of error in the estimate of value added in constant dollars. The most recent comparison of input-output coefficients for the United States used the 1947 table deflated to 1958 prices and expressed the difference in total output as the sum of two differences, one resulting from changes in final demand and one resulting from changes in the technical coefficients.[9] Using 1958 coefficients and 1947 final demand the authors calculated the 1947 output implied by the method illustrated in Set 4 of equations given above. The difference between the actual output for each industry in 1958 and the implied output in 1947 with input coefficients held constant at 1958 levels measures the share of the total difference due to final demand. The difference between the implied output in 1947, estimated from the 1947 final demand and 1958 coefficients, and the actual 1947 outputs measures changes in the input coefficients with final demand held constant.

It is apparent that the index number problem in this kind of comparison is greatly complicated. If 1947 had been selected for the base situation both for deflating and for factoring the differences in industrial output into shares explained by changes in final demand and the shares explained by changes in input coefficients, the results would all have been different. The problem is not unique to economic analysis, for standardization is the only technique the social sciences have for reducing data to measures that allow for identifying the sources of change.

Changes or differences in the input coefficients do not, in themselves, provide a measure of technological changes or differences. But the appearance of such a study is sure to stimulate research directed toward the types of technical change that could underlie the alterations in the coefficients for particular industries. It is undoubtedly safe to predict that, with tables for more years to use in comparisons, research will be directed toward association of the indicated changes in the coefficients, direct and indirect, with developments that historians of technology view as real changes in the technology. Economic historians would welcome such developments as an extension of the research on the relation of technology to economic growth, which has occupied numbers of graduate students in economic history at the

[9]*Ibid.*

University of Pennsylvania, the University of Delaware and perhaps at other graduate schools.

HISTORICAL INFERENCE

Many of the uses made of input-ouput analysis are interpretations of the relationships described by the two tables of coefficients, the inter-industry coefficients and the coefficients that measure total require-ments, direct and indirect, per unit of final demand. The tables provide the means for calculating an impressive array of statistical re-lationships. Derived tables showing how the output of particular indus-tries is related to the final demand for the products of all industries, how the price of a particular product is related to factor payments and how the output of various industries depends on imports, directly and indirectly, suggest the wide range of historical comparisons that could easily contribute to our understanding of the processes of growth and development.

Much of the vast literature on input-output systems in theory and in practice has been devoted to their use in projection and forecasting. But the quite direct use for long-range forecasting of the version of the system described here, known as the static open model, has been subject to considerable criticism. The question of whether the fore-casts and projections are better than those based on other methods has yet to be answered through empirical tests. Projections backward in time are different from projections forward in time in that the investi-gators have some actual data at their disposal. In the case of the trans-actions table, the data for the second, third and fourth quadrants can be assembled from existing sources as William Whitney did for 1899.

Projection with the input-output for a single year involves price de-flation, just as in the comparison of two or more input-output tables, followed by adjustments in the input coefficients to agree with the marginal totals given by the data from the censuses or compiled from other investigations. Now the historian wants to know what credence can be attached to inferences based on the 1899 tables adjusted to represent 1889 and 1879. Are they any better than the projections to dates in the future have proved to be? To the extent that the source data are reliable, the availability of the marginal totals for the tables should make them better. Projections to earlier periods in time could make a contribution to our knowledge of possible sources of error in projections into the future. Compilations of tables for 1879 and 1889, which will most certainly be carried through sometime and somewhere, will provide the basis for evaluation of Whitney's projections.

On the whole, the literature on the input-output analysis, theoretical and empirical, is written from the viewpoint of the student of economic history, in a foreign language that cannot easily be learned. Even with a knowledge of matrix algebra, the descriptions of the computations are, in general, unnecessarily complicated. Most of the calculations are really quite simple, either extensions of the equations illustrated in Set 3 and Set 6, taking account of the sectors of final demand or the composition of factor payments, or some kind of indexes which are weighted averages. The material in the tables is accessible to the student of economic history, once he understands the uses of the primary tables, when the titles, captions and stubs of the derived tables are given in words that describe their content. This is probably why input-output systems were included among the topics in a seminar in economic history. They will affect research in the future through the understanding historians will have of the uses that can be made of their work in the construction of the transactions matrix, and through the analyses historians will carry out with tables of input coefficients, tables of direct and indirect requirements per unit of final demand and all the tables derived from the basic three.

VIII   Specification, Quantification and Analysis in Economic History

Lance E. Davis

MY TASK is to introduce you to the "new" economic history, a supposedly different methodology. That term was coined by a former colleague, J. R. T. Hughes, almost a decade ago, and to paraphrase a typical female British writer of detective fiction, "If he had known then what he knows now he would never have turned down that narrow dark academic lane."[1]

Let me begin this talk with a heretical assertion. I do not believe that the "new" economic history is new, nor do I believe that it represents an alternative methodology. This assertion, of course, does not deny that the term has been the focus of a great number of academic wrangles, nor does it deny that a number of economic historians, including myself, have found their way to fame and fortune through their participation in this twentieth-century replay of the *Methodenstreit*.[2] It does, however, suggest that any meaningful exchange between old, new and uncommitted historians, if it ever existed, was probably over before the first article was written or the first paper read.

Still, we have to earn a living, and no one wants to abandon a good thing. If on the football field the opponents have managed to defense your long gainer, there is almost certainly a counter that can be run for additional yards, and if your girl friend has left town, there is always a bus. The route may be different, but the pay-off is still there. Therefore, I am going to sketch hurriedly the outlines of the academic battle of the past decade; I will then argue that the new

[1]The first use of the term *new economic history*, to the best of my knowledge, was in Lance E. Davis, Jonathan R. T. Hughes and Duncan M. McDougall, *American Economic History: The Development of a National Economy* (Homewood, Ill., 1961), vii.

[2]See, for example, Robert W. Fogel, "The New Economic History. I. Its Findings and Method," *Economic History Review*, 2nd ser., XIX (Dec. 1966) 642–56, and Lance E. Davis, "And It Will Never Be Literature," *Explorations in Entrepreneurial History*, 2nd ser., VI (Fall 1968), 75–92, for bibliographies of the discussion.

economic history represents no new methodology; and finally, I am going to suggest that even if it has failed to realize its full potential, it has produced, will produce or can produce some important results both for economists and for historians. Almost forty-seven years ago Sir John H. Clapham lamented "those empty economic boxes."[3] Far too many of them are still locked, if not empty; however, the new economic history, if not producing a master key, has at least yielded a somewhat inferior lock pick. It is on these contributions that I want to focus attention. Finally, if nothing else, this paper is aimed at convincing historians that causal statements imply some theory, and economists that a regression equation is not a theory.

The new economic history is not new, or at least not very new. The fact that it is largely quantitative does not make it new. There has always been quantification in economic history. The fact that it attempts to explain economic phenomena in terms of certain independent economic and sometimes noneconomic variables does not make it new, for that is what economic historians have been doing for decades. And the fact that it depends on the application of theory to problems of explanation does not make it new, because that too has been a part of traditional economic history. If it differs at all from more traditional work, and here I must argue that it does, it is because it makes explicit use of theory. In the past, historians have always made use of theoretical arguments, but all too frequently they have failed to expose their assumptions and the chain of reasoning that led from assumptions to conclusions. The new history is nothing but an attempt formally to introduce scientific method to the study of historical social science phenomena. Thus far, the work has largely been limited to economic history, but that limitation is a result of lack of adequate theory in sociology, political science and psychology, not because the method is inherently inappropriate to these fields.

Despite the protestations of more traditional historians that theory is of no value and that they never use it themselves, there are few pieces of economic or other types of history that do not lean heavily upon theory. In the absence of theory (implicit or explicit), history would be limited to classification and description, and I know of no historian who would willingly accept that limitation. If a historian

[3]Clapham, "Of Empty Economic Boxes," *Economic Journal*, XXXII (Sept. 1922), 305–14.

asserts that "the invention of the printing press made an important contribution to the development of the modern world," he has argued that there is some relation between a particular invention and the process of social and economic change. Moreover, he has asserted that the world would have been different had the invention not been made. In short, he has made a theoretical proposition of the form: *A* implies *B* and *A*. What he has not done is to spell out the assumptions that must be made if one is to argue that *A* implies *B*, nor has he shown how he has deduced that conclusion from whatever axioms and premises he has used. The reader, then, is left with an assertion that he has no way of evaluating. He cannot tell what assumptions he has been asked to accept, nor can he discover if the historian has done his arithmetic correctly.

It has been argued that those who view history as an art are really stating that the historian has a unique ability to derive valid deductions from relevant theories without making the nature of this process known to anyone, including himself. If this is true, the word *art* does not refer to an aesthetic appeal but is only a pseudonym for a special form of witchcraft. The new economic history is designed to remove this aspect of witchcraft from the writing of history, and everyone wants to do away with witches except, perhaps, the witches themselves. Witchcraft is particularly prevalent in four areas of historical research.

First, if one is going to argue that *A* implies *B*, it is necessary that both *A* and *B* be defined in an operational manner. That is, the terms must be defined so that an independent observer can see *A* if it is present and can, in theory at least, note the presence of *B* even if *A* is not observed. This requirement may not sound very revolutionary, but traditional economic history is heavily populated by terms and concepts that have no operational counterpart.

For example, in American history, the explanation of the pattern of western settlement has largely been written in terms of the behavior of speculators. Many historians have concluded that things would have been better had public policy been directed toward the elimination of speculators.[4] In terms of theory, the argument asserts

[4]See, for example, Paul W. Gates, "The Role of the Land Speculator in Western Development," *Pennsylvania Magazine of History and Biography*, LXVI (1942), 314–33, or Harry N. Scheiber, "State Policy and the Public Domain: The Ohio Canal Lands," *Journal of Economic History*, XXV (March 1965), 86–113.

that the presence of speculators biased the pattern of settlement in a manner that was unfavorable to American growth and that appropriate policy would have altered the pattern in some desirable manner. No one, however, has ever defined the term *speculator* in a way that is operational within the context of the theory. In the absence of any historically applicable techniques of motivational analysis, it is unlikely that they ever will. Instead, historians have implicitly defined a speculator as anyone whose actions cause settlement patterns to deviate from those that the historians would prefer, and a nonspeculator as anyone whose actions do not lead to this result. Given these definitions, no one can quarrel with their conclusions, but one may certainly wonder about the usefulness of their results.

Again, a great deal of British economic history is focused on attempts to explain the cause and to measure the impact of the Industrial Revolution. Nowhere, however, is the term defined in an operational manner. As a result, it is possible for a distinguished agricultural historian to argue within a single article that (1) a period of rising farm prices caused the Industrial Revolution; (2) a period of falling farm prices caused the Industrial Revolution; and (3) a period of stable farm prices caused the Industrial Revolution. Since the term is undefined, it can be caused by anything.

Compare these nonoperational definitions with some of the more precise definitions adopted by the new economic historians. Allen and Margaret Bogue and Robert P. Swierenga have defined speculators as persons who purchase large blocks of land.[5] This definition is operational and permits them to make certain testable assertions about the group and its impact on the economy. It is, however, nonmotivational and cannot be used as a basis for any causal argument relating motivation to the pattern of settlement. Robert W. Fogel defines excessive profits as profits larger than those required to compensate investors for a risky investment and provides an operational technique for determining that level.[6] Although the term was frequently used previously, it was never defined; and a profit that appeared excessive

---

[5]Bogue and Bogue, " 'Profits' and the Frontier Land Speculator," *Journal of Economic History*, XVII, No. 1 (1957), 1–24; Swierenga, "Land Speculator 'Profits' Reconsidered: Central Iowa as a Test Case," *ibid.*, XXVI (March 1966), 1–28.

[6]Fogel, *The Union Pacific Railroad: A Case of Premature Enterprise* (Baltimore, 1960).

to me may have appeared quite normal to someone else. In both cases, the definitions preclude certain questions. But given these definitions, an independent observer can tell whether or not there were speculators and excess profits. With operational definitions the historian can proceed to the explicit formulation of his theory—a theory that becomes, in principle, operational itself.

Second, from the theory it is possible for the historian to deduce the nature of the counterfactual world. That is, prediction or understanding involves the comparison of the world as it exists with a world that would have existed had the causal agent not been present. Since that world never existed, it cannot be observed. It can only be described in terms of the theoretical model, and its description will change with the model employed. This fact should be obvious in the case of historical phenomena. After all, history only happened in one way. But even in science use is made of the concept of an ideal experiment.

The recent controversy between Robert W. Fogel, Albert Fishlow and Stanley Lebergott over the size of the social savings attributable to the innovation of the railroads is a good example of alternative models leading to alternative counterfactual worlds, and those worlds in turn leading to vastly different assessments of the phenomena under consideration.[7] In fact, Fogel concludes that the railroads were not indispensable to American growth in 1890; Fishlow that they were not indispensable in 1859, but they were in 1890; and Lebergott that they were indispensable even in 1859. There is no way of choosing the correct model; in fact, there is no correct model. If, however, the alternative theories are fully specified, the reader can choose the one he wants to accept. In the social savings example, Lebergott's conclusions are postulated on the assumption that any transport network would operate at capacity, despite the fact that even today there is insufficient traffic to achieve capacity operation of the network that existed in the mid-nineteenth century. One might, therefore, conclude that his model, although logically consistent, contributes little to the discussion.

[7]Fogel, *Railroads and American Economic Growth: Essays in Econometric History* (Baltimore, 1964); Fishlow, *American Railroads and the Transformation of the Antebellum Economy* (Cambridge, Mass., 1965); Lebergott, "United States Transport Advance and Externalities," *Journal of Economic History*, XXVI (Dec. 1966), 437–461.

Again, Lawrence A. Harper and Douglass C. North have disagreed about the impact of the Navigation Acts on the colonial economy.[8] This disagreement stems from the counterfactual world that each has chosen as his yardstick against which to compare the actual economy of 1770. Harper argues that the colonies without the Navigation Acts would have looked like the United States in the years from 1820 to 1840, and this comparison indicates the Acts were quite detrimental. North, on the other hand, asserts that the relevant counterfactual is typified by the United States from 1785 to 1793 and that a comparison indicates the burden was at most quite negligible. There is, of course, no correct counterfactual. There never was a colonial America of 1770 without the Navigation Acts. But in this instance the problem is even more difficult. Neither author spells out the model he has used to relate the Acts to the level of output, if, in fact, either has an explicit model. The reader has little basis for choosing between the alternatives. It is only with an explicit model that the reader can learn what characteristics the counterfactual world possesses and what assumptions are necessary to give it these characteristics and, therefore, have any reasonable basis for deciding whether it is the United States in 1785–93, in 1820–40 or in 1960–68 that provides the best proxy.

In sum, if one wants to explain the British industrial revolution in terms of movements in agricultural prices, one needs not only to define terms operationally but also to specify a model that relates such prices to changes in the now defined revolution. Anything less is gibberish.

Third, operational definitions and a well-specified theory can contribute to our understanding of history only if the initial conditions are met in the real world. In simpler terms, any theory can yield implications, but they can become predictive only if the theory has at least some vague connection with the world that it is attempting to predict. The selection of appropriate theories is, of course, merely another name for the specification problem that Professor Fogel has discussed so thoroughly.[9] Lebergott's model is probably inappropri-

[8]Harper, "The Effects of the Navigation Acts on the Thirteen Colonies," in Richard Brandon Morris (ed.), *The Era of the American Revolution* (New York, 1939); North, *Growth and Welfare in the American Past* (Englewood Cliffs, N.J., 1966).

[9]Fogel, "The Specification Problem in Economic History," *Journal of Economic History*, XXVII (Sept. 1967), 283–308.

ate in a discussion of nineteenth-century transport, since its assumptions are not met even in the mid-twentieth century. Traditional historians have tended not to specify their models, and the reader is left with no basis on which to discriminate. In the literature of the new economic history, however, there is a tendency for its practitioners to misspecify their model. This is hardly a lesser error. It is, in fact, so important that I would like to turn to it again later in this paper.

Fourth, and finally, the economic historian must compare the counterfactual world deduced from his model with the world as it actually exists. This comparison, if the model is correctly specified, should show the impact of the causal factor, and here most frequently the new historian turns to quantification and measurement. There is, of course, no necessary reason for the comparison to be limited to manipulation of traditionally quantitative evidence. Alfred H. Conrad and John R. Meyer, for example, are able to conclude that slavery was economically viable only by comparing the actual rate of return on investment in slaves with the return that could have been earned on some hypothetical alternative portfolio.[10] These alternative investments were never undertaken, and no one will ever know whether the ones selected were indeed the correct ones. If Fogel's study of the railroads' impact on American growth is to be faulted, it is because he never completes the formal comparison between the real world and the counterfactual world that he has so carefully deduced. On the other hand, his work in the area of measurement is at its best when he compares the actual profits earned by the Union Pacific with the hypothetical return needed to induce investment into so risky a project. In my work on the capital markets, measurement takes the form of comparing actual interest rates in various regions with the hypothetical returns that would have prevailed in a world of free capital movements and of comparing changes in regional differentials with the diffusion of capital market institutions.[11]

These four steps then, (1) operational definitions, (2) explicit theory leading to explicit counterfactual states, (3) careful specification of that theory to conform with the actual initial conditions and

[10]Conrad and Meyer, "The Economics of Slavery in the Ante Bellum South," *Journal of Political Economy*, LXVI (Feb. 1958), 95–130.

[11]Davis, "The Investment Market, 1870–1914: The Evolution of a National Market," *Journal of Economic History*, XXV (Sept. 1965), 355–99.

(4) measurement leading to a comparison of the actual world with the deduced counterfactual world, describe the methodology of the new economic history. In actuality, it differs little from more traditional economic history except that at each stage the procedure is formalized and the assumptions underlying the theory are made explicit. At its best, it has yielded some important new results, but not all of the work represents the methodology at its best. Moreover, the very tightness of the method has tended to constrain its application both temporally and, perhaps more important, in terms of the questions it has asked.

I do not think this paper is the place to describe at length the positive contributions of the new economic history, but it does appear appropriate to mention a few before turning to an examination of its faults. The change in our view of Southern history that has followed Conrad and Meyer's study of slavery has already been impressed on the pages of the standard history texts, and almost everyone recognizes that the dominant position in the history of American development formerly given to the railroad has at the very least been threatened by the findings of Robert Fogel. Less well known, but in many ways equally important, are the revisions of our history of the 1930s that are dictated by the findings of E. Cary Brown and the revision of our views of the role of the Interstate Commerce Commission that, though it has yet to find its way into the textbooks, must follow from the work of Paul W. MacAvoy.[12] The errors, both of commission and omission, in the new history are, however, at least as numerous. In particular, it appears useful to dwell on three sources of trouble that have been largely responsible for the failure of the methodology to realize its full potential.

First, to return to an earlier theme, is the question of proper specification. Many of the young and not so young men who masquerade as new economic historians are very clever chaps; however, all too frequently they have displayed a willingness to put cleverness ahead of common sense. The result has often been badly misspecified models which, while yielding any number of predictive implications, contribute little to our understanding of the past. In short, they

---

[12]Brown, "Fiscal Policy in the 'Thirties: A Reappraisal," *American Economic Review*, XLVI (Dec. 1956), 857–79; MacAvoy, *The Economic Effects of Regulation* (Cambridge, Mass., 1965).

have chosen to use models that are so unlike the world they are trying to explain that their implications cloud rather than illuminate our understanding.

Paul A. David, for example, employs a very clever economic model to argue that the rapid innovation of the reaper in the mid-nineteenth century was a product not only of the increasing relative cost of labor but also of increases in the demand for wheat.[13] This result, however, depends on his assumption that the services of a reaper are indivisible. Given the state of reaper technology at the time, it is certainly possible that the reaper was mechanically indivisible. Mechanical indivisibility is not, however, the same as indivisibility of its services. It is easy to conceive of firms specializing in the sale of reaper services or groups of farmers jointly owning a reaper. Either arrangement could yield any desired degree of divisibility of service. Moreover, a reading of nineteenth-century history shows that both such arrangements were quite common. As a result, David's model, though worth an *A* for cleverness, does little to further our understanding of nineteenth-century American agricultural history.

Again, in a recent article Peter Temin has provided a formal, if not revolutionary, analysis of relative factor intensities in nineteenth-century British and American technology.[14] From his analysis he concludes that American technology was less capital intensive than British and that real wages were lower in the United States than they were in the United Kingdom. His model is logically impeccable, but a careful examination of that model indicates that these quite amazing conclusions rest on some equally amazing assumptions. In order to simplify his analysis, Temin assumes that while there are three factors of production, land, labor, and capital, only two, land and labor, are used in agriculture, and only two, capital and labor, are used in manufacturing. Putting aside the question of agriculture, even a cursory glance at early nineteenth-century history indicates that the bulk of American manufacturing was devoted to the processing of agricultural commodities. Thus, under no set of reasonable assumptions can land be left out of the manufacturing production function, and if it is included it is no longer possible to deduce Temin's more

[13]David, "The Mechanization of Reaping in the Ante Bellum Mid-West," in Henry Rosovsky (ed.), *Industrialization in Two Systems* (New York, 1966).

[14]Temin, "Labor Scarcity and the Problems of American Industrial Efficiency," *Journal of Economic History*, XXVI (Sept. 1966), 277–98.

dramatic results.[15] Proper specification is important. Without it, the models, no matter how elaborate, contribute little to our understanding of economic history.

Second, among the causes of the disappointing performance of the new economic history has been the failure of theory to provide models relevant to many of the most important questions. Ignoring the problems engendered by the almost total failure of sociology and political science to produce operationally useful models of any sort, the present state of economic theory is inadequate to support work in many important areas in economic history. On the plus side, however, in a few cases history has suggested some modifications in traditional theory and has, perhaps, pointed toward an ultimate solution. As long as work is devoted to questions amenable to analysis with static price theory or simple models of income determination, theory has provided no barrier to work in the new economic history. Economists have long argued that you can go a long way with supply and demand, and the recent controversy between Leland H. Jenks, Temin and Fogel over the innovation of mineral fuel in western Pennsylvania suggests that the old adage is still true.[16] Similarly, Brown's reappraisal of New Deal fiscal policy shows just how much mileage there is in a simple Keynesian model.

When, however, we consider questions that are not amenable to such analysis, and particularly when we turn to problems of long-term growth and change, the lack of adequate theory becomes quickly apparent. Most growth theory takes as given both the number of firms and the institutional arrangements between firms. Such theory is not very helpful in understanding change in a world characterized by entry and exit and rapidly altering institutional arrangements. Moreover, what little oligopoly theory there is continues to be focused on short-run decisions. It offers very little to an understanding of an oligopolist's behavior, particularly an oligopolist who is partially protected from competition, when the firm must choose some optimal growth path and when information is not costless and uncertainties are high. Finally, if the questions involve the decisions of government and other bureaucracies, institutions that buy inputs but do not

---

[15]This criticism is neatly spelled out in Fogel's "Specification."

[16]Robert W. Fogel and Stanley Engerman (eds.), *American Economic History, A Reinterpretation*, forthcoming.

sell outputs, theory provides little help since the work on nonmarket decision-making is in a very early stage.

Despite the relatively dismal showing of the past, recent interaction of theory and history, or at least empirical economics, has produced some steps in the direction of a more dynamic theory. On the question of entry, Vernon L. Smith, in his study of the fishing industry, has made the rate of entry and exit a function of profit differentials, and he has got some interesting results.[17] If models of this type have a more general applicability, it may be possible for economic historians to examine the growth of particular industries in a systematic fashion. Moreover, these models may permit us better to explain the widespread phenomena of secular retardation.

Progress has also been made in the area of institutional change. Although institutional economics outside the state of Texas was largely destroyed in the 1930s by the combined impact of the Keynesian and Hicks-Robinson-Chamberlin revolutions, traditional economic historians have displayed a continued interest in institutions. Although this interest has frequently made the "old" historians the butt of snide jokes by their "new" colleagues, the interest has not been misplaced. From their association with long-term change, the traditional historians recognized that institutions did have something to do with the speed and pattern of growth, a conclusion that better-trained economists have only gradually adopted. Unfortunately, there was no theory to help them understand the phenomena of institutional change, and their work has been largely descriptive and classificatory. Although the focus was initially elsewhere, recent work in theory appears to have some applicability to this problem, and some new economic historians have begun to lay the groundwork for a theory of institutional change.

The work in theory has come from two sources. On the one hand, an interest in welfare and the problem of externalities has rekindled an interest in alternative organizational forms.[18] On the other hand, work in information theory has suggested that information does have a

[17]Vernon Smith, "Economics of Production from Natural Resources," *American Economic Review*, LVIII (June 1968), 409–31.

[18]Kenneth Arrow, "Political and Economic Evaluation of Social Effects and Externalities," National Bureau of Economic Research Conference on Economics of Public Output, mimeographed (1968).

cost and that in the absence of free information, markets do not work easily.[19]

James Buchanan and Gordon Tullock, for example, have argued that when externalities exist there are economic pressures to rearrange the existing institutions in order to internalize these externalities. Moreover, they argue that the structure of the new institution will depend in part upon the numbers involved and upon the state of property rights. If numbers are small and if property rights have not been vested, the organization is likely to be a voluntary cooperative one. Although there will be organizational costs, those will be the only ones. If, on the other hand, numbers are large and/or property rights represent a substantial barrier, the new institution will most often involve the participation of government. In this instance, the costs of having to accept a decision that you do not like are less than the revenues gained from the power of government to coerce recalcitrants.

Kenneth Arrow, among others, has focused attention on the costs of information and the effect of such costs on the operation of markets. He has shown that there are potential profits that can be earned if institutional reorganization can reduce information costs. Moreover, Arrow argues that information is subject to increasing returns, and one would then expect the reorganization to produce a new institution.

Douglass North and I have drawn on this literature and have derived a loose model which we feel makes a substantial contribution to the understanding of the process of economic change on both a historical and a theoretical level.[20] Specifically, we have built a lagged supply model where the existence of potential profits external to the existing institutional arrangement induces after a lag an institutional innovation that will effect an internalizing of those external profits. The sources of potential profits include not only classic externalities and those accruing from positive information costs but those arising from technical economies of scale and those inherent in simple income redistribution. Given the size of the potential profit, the numbers of persons involved, current property rights, the tolerance of existing institutions for ambiguity and the state of institu-

[19]James M. Buchanan and Gordon Tullock, *The Calculus of Consent* (Ann Arbor, Mich., 1962).

[20]Davis and North, *Towards a Theory of Institutional Change*, forthcoming.

tional technology, the model is supposed to predict the type of institution that will emerge, i.e., voluntary, cooperative or government, and the length of lag between profit and institution.

Although the results are far from perfect and the model is still only loosely specified, it has proved useful in furthering our understanding of the rise of capital-market institutions, the growth of government regulation in the transport industry and institutional innovation in the agricultural sector, including both the Grange and the extension programs. It is hoped that further work along these lines will, for the first time, permit economists and economic historians to talk meaningfully about the process of economic growth.

On the question of oligopoly behavior, it appears that even more progress has been made. Vernon Smith's experimental results and the theoretical work of Daniel Orr and Paul MacAvoy have greatly contributed to our understanding of short-term cartel behavior.[21] Moreover, MacAvoy, in his work on the origins of the Interstate Commerce Commission, has successfully applied his theoretical notions to a historical problem.[22]

As far as long-term behavior is concerned, it is the economic historians who have led the way, but economists have begun to follow. Concern with the failure of economics to predict the long-run behavior of so much of American industry led entrepreneurial historians like Arthur Cole and Hugh Aitken to focus on the role of the decision-maker and corporate historians like Alfred Chandler to concern themselves with corporate structure and strategy.[23] Although entrepreneurial history has produced few important results, Chandler's work has been fruitful. Not only has it provided economic history with some important insights, but it has had a theoretical impact that is reflected in Richard M. Cyert and James G. March's studies of firms in relatively nonprogressive industries and the work in rapidly changing industries by Edwin Mansfield, Burton Klein and P. W. S. Andrews and Bela Gold.[24] In each case, the thrust of

---

[21]Orr and MacAvoy, "Price Strategies to Promote Cartel Stability," *Economica*, XXXII (May 1965), 186–97.

[22]MacAvoy, *Regulation*.

[23]Chandler, *Strategy and Structure: Chapters in the History of American Industrial Enterprise* (Cambridge, Mass., 1962).

[24]Richard M. Cyert and James G. March, *A Behavioral Theory of the Firm* (Englewood Cliffs, N.J., 1963).

the revisionist argument recognizes that factors internal to the firm's organization affect an oligopolist's long-term behavior. The work is far from complete, but a start has been made and we should look for further applications in the field of economic history.

Finally, lack of theory in the area of nonmarket decision-making has further restricted the scope of the new economic history. As one moves nearer and nearer to the present, the role of government and other bureaucratic institutions gets larger and larger. Any attempt at understanding the behavior of these institutions must rest on a theory of nonmarket decision-making. Any such theory must explain at least two types of phenomena. First, it is necessary to understand the political process, since many decisions rest on some interaction of the political structure and the electorate. Second, it is necessary to understand the process of small-group decision-making, since many bureaucratic decisions are made by committees.

In this area, which might better be classified as political science or political economy, the first steps toward formal theory have been taken. Anthony Downs has modified Harold Hotelling's model of economic location and has used it to analyze the behavior of political parties.[25] In a more recent work, he has also provided some intriguing suggestions about the process of bureaucratic decision-making.[26] Along slightly different lines, Otto A. Davis has begun to model committee decisions both in Congress and at the local level.[27] These are all tentative steps that will be reflected in further work in the new economic history.

In addition to the misspecification and lack of adequate theory, the new economic history has suffered from a lack of historical data. This lack shows up in two ways. First, it limits the total quantity of work done, and second, it provides a temporal bias toward periods with good data such as the present. In part, the data shortage reflects the natural laziness of theoretically minded new economic historians who have never been convinced of the need for basic re-

---

[25]Anthony Downs, *An Economic Theory of Democracy* (New York, 1957), see also Gordon Tullock, *Toward a Mathematics of Politics* (Ann Arbor, Mich., 1967).

[26]Downs, *Inside Bureaucracy* (Boston, 1967).

[27]Otto A. Davis, M. A. H. Dempster and Aaron Wildavsky, "A Theory of the Budgetary Process," *American Political Science Review,* LX (Sept. 1966), 529–47, and "On the Process of Budgeting: An Empirical Study of Congressional Appropriation," in Gordon Tullock (ed.), *Papers on Non-Market Decision Making,* I (1966), 63–132.

search in economic history. (Another extreme case is a well-known member of the profession who boasts that he will never use data from an unpublished source.) In part, however, the scarcity of data is a function of the new questions that have been asked and the quite different type of evidence that is needed to answer them. Much of the work of traditional economic historians has been addressed to different questions, and the evidence they have adduced is of limited usefulness to the new history. This limitation is particularly binding in the case of most but not all business history. In the future, however, firm records should become an important source of evidence; and business history with a slightly different focus, history of the kind written by Harold F. Williamson, for example, ought to become an important resource for any new economic historian.[28] We are now and have always been, after all, a business economy.

This then is the current state of the art. The "new" history is exciting, infuriating and very interesting.

[28]See, for example, Harold F. Williamson and Orange A. Smalley, *Northwestern Mutual Life* (Evanston, Ill., 1957).

Bibliography

Lucius F. Ellsworth

THE following list is intended to guide students to representative books and articles about various approaches to economic history. Each section is divided into two parts: the first contains an annotated list of essays that discuss the approach, and the second part cites examples of the application of the approach to specific historical problems. Through these materials it is hoped that the interested reader will gain a better understanding of the evolution of some of the rich methodological discussions concerning economic history.

Business history occupied a prominent position in the original seminar series. Although the subsequent illness of the lecturer on business history prevented the publication of a revised paper in this volume, the editors decided to prepare reading lists for each of the original nine topics. They believed that to omit business history was to delete a substantial and important body of scholarship with which the student should become familiar.

The reader should observe that overlapping in subject matter does exist among several topics, e.g., entrepreneurial, institutional and sociological history or statistical and input and output analysis. Because it seemed desirable to select only those basic materials that would be fairly accessible to the beginning graduate student, many helpful foreign publications were necessarily excluded. No effort to construct a comprehensive bibliography of American titles has been made.

BUSINESS HISTORY

Cole, Arthur H. "Aggregative Business History," *Business History Review*, XXXIX (Autumn 1965), 287–300. An interesting attempt to synthesize the historical study of entrepreneurship and business by a student of both approaches.

————. "Business History and Economic History," Supplement V of *Journal of Economic History*, V (Dec. 1945), 45–53. Encourages business historians to seek answers to different types of questions so that business and economic history might be more closely related.

_____. "What Is Business History?," *Business History Review*, XXXVI (Spring 1962), 98–107. Another effort to persuade business historians to enlarge their fields of study.

Galambos. Louis. *American Business History*. American Historical Association Publication no. 70. Washington D.C., 1967. A review of the writing of business history in the United States to the mid-1960s with a discussion of some of the more influential publications.

_____. "Business History and the Theory of the Growth of the Firm," *Explorations in Entrepreneurial History*, 2nd ser., IV (Fall 1966), 3–16. Suggests ways of integrating microeconomics, particularly theories of the growth of the firm, into the study of business organization in history.

Krooss, Herman E. "Economic History and the New Business History," and Lance Davis, "Discussion," *Journal of Economic History*, XVIII (Dec. 1958), 467–85. An analysis of the "revisionist" business histories written in the late 1940s and 1950s which stresses both the contributions and the significant shortcomings of this new approach.

Larson, H. M. *Guide to Business History*. Cambridge, Mass., 1948, 3–19. A sketch of the development of business history as a discipline in Europe and the United States to the mid-1930s.

Redlich, Fritz. "Approaches to Business History" and "Comments," *Business History Review*, XXXVI (Spring 1962), 61–86. A critical evaluation of the lack of theory in business history and a statement of the relationship of business history to economic history.

Williamson, Harold F. "Business History and Economic History," *Journal of Economic History*, XXVI (Dec. 1966), 407–17. Suggests the "extent to which business history is part and parcel of economic history" yet still maintains a separate identity.

Examples

Johnson, Arthur M. *The Development of American Petroleum Pipelines: A Study in Private Enterprise and Public Policy, 1862–1906*. Ithaca, N.Y. 1956.

Larson, Henrietta. *Jay Cooke, Private Banker*. Cambridge, Mass., 1936.

Overton, Richard C. *Burlington Route: A History of the Burlington Lines*. New York, 1965.

Salsbury, Stephen. *The State, the Investor, and the Railroad: The Boston & Albany, 1825–1867*. Cambridge, Mass., 1967.

Williamson, Harold F., and Orange A. Smalley. *Northwestern Mutual Life: A Century of Trusteeship*. Evanston, Ill., 1957.

ENTREPRENEURIAL APPROACH

Cole, Arthur H. "An Approach to the Study of Entrepreneurship: A Tribute to Edwin F. Gay," *The Tasks of Economic History*, Supplement VI of *Journal of Economic History*, VI (Dec. 1946), 1–15; reprinted in Hugh G. J. Aitken, *Explorations in Enterprise* (Cambridge, Mass., 1965), 45–64 (hereinafter cited as Aitken, *Explorations*). A different approach to entrepreneurial studies.

_____. "Meso-Economics: A Contribution from Entrepreneurial History," *Explorations in Enterpreneurial History*, 2nd ser., VI (Fall 1968), 3–33. An attempt to make theories of entrepreneurial activity relevant to the study of economic change and the business system.

Galambos, Louis. *American Business History*. American Historical Association Publication no. 70. Washington, D.C., 1967, 20–25. A summary of the major contributions of entrepreneurial history to the mid-1960s.

Schumpeter, Joseph A. "The Creative Response in Economic History," *Journal of Economic History*, VII (Nov. 1947), 149–59. A concise statement of his theory of creative response or innovation and its relevance to the study of economic history.

_____. "Economic Theory and Enterpreneurial History," in *Change and the Entrepreneur*. Cambridge, Mass., 1949, 63–84; reprinted in Aitken, *Explorations*, 45–64. Traces the antecedents of entrepreneurial history and defines entrepreneurship.

Sawyer, John E. "Entrepreneurial Studies: Perspectives and Directions, 1948–1958," *Business History Review*, XXXII (Winter 1958), 434–43. A review of the work of the Research Center in Entrepreneurial History which Arthur H. Cole founded and guided at Harvard University.

Symposium on "The Entrepreneur" in *American Economic Review*, LVIII (May 1968), 60–92: Arthur H. Cole, "Introductory Remarks"; William J. Baumol, "Entrepreneurship in Economic Theory"; Harvey Leibenstein, "Entrepreneurship and Development"; James H. Soltow, "The Entrepreneur in Economic History." A discussion of the usefulness of the entrepreneurial models in understanding economic phenomena.

Thomas, Robert Paul. "The Automobile Industry and Its Tycoon," *Explorations in Entrepreneurial History*, 2nd ser., VI (Winter 1969), 139–57. A sharp criticism of the entrepreneurial approach to history by a practitioner of the new economic history.

Examples

Aitken, Hugh G. J. *Taylorism at Watertown Arsenal: Scientific Management in Action, 1908–15*. Cambridge, Mass., 1960.

Passer, Harold. *The Electrical Manufacturers, 1875–1900*. Cambridge, Mass., 1953.

Sawyer, John E. "Strains in the Social Structure of Modern France," in
    Edward M. Earle (ed.), *Modern France*. Princeton, N.J., 1951, 293–
    312.

INSTITUTIONAL HISTORY

Chandler, Alfred D., Jr. *Strategy and Structure: Chapters in the History of
    the Industrial Enterprise*. Cambridge, Mass., 1962, esp. 1–18 and
    380–96. Chandler develops the thesis "that different organizational
    forms result from different types of growth."
Devereux, Edward C., Jr. "Parsons' Sociological Theory," in Max Black
    (ed.), *The Social Theories of Talcott Parsons*. Englewood Cliffs, N.J.,
    1961. 1–63. A summary of the theories of the Harvard sociologist who
    influenced such economic historians as Alfred Chandler and Thomas C.
    Cochran, both participants in the Research Center in Entrepreneurial
    History.
Gerth, H. H., and C. Wright Mills (eds.). "Bureaucracy," in *Max Weber:
    Essays in Sociology*. New York, 1965, 196–244. A statement of one of
    the theories frequently used as the conceptual framework of the pres-
    ent-day institutionalists.
Gruchy, Allan G. "Economic Thought: The Institutional School," in David
    L. Sills (ed.), *International Encyclopedia of the Social Sciences*. New
    York, 1968, IV, 462–67. A sketch of the approach developed by the
    institutional economists of the early twentieth century in reaction to
    neoclassical economic theory, pointing out that, although leading prac-
    tioners of institutional history today derive most of their theories from
    sociology, they analyze many of the same institutions as their prede-
    cessors did.
Schumpeter, Joseph A. *Business Cycles: A Theoretical, Historical, and
    Statistical Analysis of the Capitalist Process*. New York, 1964. The
    best statement of his theory.

Examples

Chandler, Alfred D., Jr. "The Beginnings of 'Big Business' in American
    Industry," *Business History Review*, XXXIII (Spring 1959), 1–31.
———. "The Large Industrial Corporation and the Making of the Modern
    American Economy," in Stephen Ambrose (ed.), *Institutions in Modern
    America*. Baltimore, 1967, 71–101
Chandler, Alfred D., Jr., and Louis Galambos. "The Development of Large-
    Scale Economic Organizations in Modern America," *Journal of Eco-
    nomic History*, XXX (March 1970), 201–17.

Galambos, Louis. *Competition and Cooperation: The Emergence of a National Trade Association*. Baltimore, 1966.

Hurst, James Willard. *Law and Economic Growth: The Legal History of the Lumber Industry in Wisconsin, 1836–1915*. Cambridge, Mass., 1964.

STAGE THEORIES

Baran, Paul, and Ernest Hobshawm. "The Stages of Economic Growth: A Review," *Kyklos*, XIV (1961), 234–42. Also available in Gerald D. Nash (ed.), *Issues in American Economic History* (Boston, 1964), 540–49. A slashing attack on the Rostow doctrine from a Marxist viewpoint.

Fishlow, Albert. "Empty Economic Stages?" *Economic Journal*, LXXV (March 1965), 112–25. An "evaluation of the economic and historical adequacy of the take-off and stage theory."

Gras, N. S. B. "Stages in Economic History," *Journal of Economic and Business History*, II (May 1930), 395–418. A general survey and appraisal of early stage theories.

Hoselitz, Bert F. "Theories of Stages of Economic Growth," in Bert F. Hoselitz (ed.), *Theories of Economic Growth*. Glencoe, Ill., 1960, 193–238. Especially valuable for its summary of the stage theories of the German school.

Ohlin, Goran. "Reflections on the Rostow Doctrine," *Economic Development and Cultural Change*, IX (July 1961), 648–55. An early review of Rostow's major work.

Rosovsky, Henry. "The Take-Off into Sustained Controversy," *Journal of Economic History*, XXV (June 1965), 271–75. Review of the following book which includes an indication of the position which each member of the conference at Konstanz, Germany, in 1963 took on the Rostow doctrine.

Rostow, W. W. (ed.). *The Economics of Take-Off into Sustained Growth*. New York, 1965. Report of a conference held at Konstanz, Germany, in 1963 at which leading economic historians analyzed the Rostow theory. Rostow was given an opportunity to reply. The essays are indispensable for the student who wishes to explore the objections to and defense of Rostow's position.

Examples

Clark, Colin. *The Conditions of Economic Progress*. London, 1940.

Cole, Arthur H. "A New Set of Stages," *Explorations in Entrepreneurial History*, VIII (Dec. 1955), 99–107.

Gras, N. S. B. *An Introduction to Economic History.* New York, 1922.

Hoffmann, Walther G. *The Growth of Industrial Economies.* New York, 1958.

Rostow, W. W. "Industrialization and Economic Growth," in *First International Conference of Economic History*, Stockholm, 1960 (Paris–The Hague, 1960), 17–34.

——. *The Process of Economic Growth.* 2nd ed. Oxford, 1960.

——. *The Stages of Economic Growth: A Non-Communist Manifesto.* Cambridge, Eng., 1960.

Slichter, Sumner H. *Economic Growth in the United States: Its History, Problems, and Prospects.* Baton Rouge, La., 1961, esp. chapter II.

ECONOMIC INTERPRETATION

Beard, Charles A. *An Economic Interpretation of the Constitution of the United States.* New York, 1913, 1–18. Reasons for employing the economic interpretation of the Constitution and the limits of this approach.

Benson, Lee. *Turner and Beard: American Historical Writing Reconsidered.* Glencoe, Ill., 1960, 95–228. An essentially hostile evaluation of Beard's major works.

Dobb, Maurice. *"Economic Thought: Socialist Thought,"* in David L. Sills (ed.), *International Encyclopedia of the Social Sciences.* New York, 1968, IV, 446–54. Short summary of development of socialist thought to the mid-1960s.

Dorfman, Joseph. *The Economic Mind in American Civilization.* New York, 1949, III, 345–51. A summarization of various economic interpretations of history.

Fromm, Erich. *Marx's Concept of Man.* New York, 1961. Acute statements on the Marxist's view of man.

Hofstadter, Richard. *The Progressive Historians: Turner, Beard, Parrington.* New York, 1968, esp. parts 4–14. Relatively favorable essays analyzing Beard's and Turner's interpretations of history.

McDonald, Forrest. *We The People: The Economic Origins of the Constitution.* Chicago, 1958, 349–417. Suggests that although Beard's approach was inadequate, economic factors do help to explain the drafting of the Constitution.

Seligman, Edwin R. A. *The Economic Interpretation of History.* New York, 1902. A history to the end of the nineteenth century of the development of the economic approach with an evaluation of its usefulness.

Shoup, Carl S. "Edwin R. A. Seligman," in David L. Sills (ed.), *International Encyclopedia of the Social Sciences.* New York, 1968, XIV, 163–64. A short biographical sketch.

Taylor, Overton H. *A History of Economic Thought.* New York, 1960, 271–309. An analysis of the socialist, Hegelian and Ricardian elements in Karl Marx's thought.

Examples

Beard, Charles A. *An Economic Interpretation of the Constitution of the United States.* New York, 1913.

Beard, Charles A. and Mary R. *The Rise of American Civilization.* New York, 1927.

Marx, Karl, and Frederick Engels. *The Communist Manifesto.* Ed. Samuel H. Beer. New York, 1955.

SOCIOLOGICAL APPROACH

Biddle, Bruce J., and Edwin J. Thomas (eds.). *Role Theory; Concepts and Research.* New York, 1966. An extended discussion of the concept of role theory.

Cochran, Thomas C. "Economic History, Old and New," *American Historical Review,* LXXIV (June 1969), esp. 1569–72. Suggests the usefulness of using verbal and modal models.

_____. *The Inner Revolution.* New York, 1964, particularly chapters II, VI, VII and X. A collection of essays which surveys the application of social science theories to the study of history, particularly economic history, and advances a model for explaining cultural factors.

_____. "Role and Sanction in American Entrepreneural History," in *Change and the Entrepreneur.* Cambridge, Mass., 1949, 153–75. Reprinted in Hugh G. J. Aitken, *Explorations in Enterprise* (Cambridge, 1965), 93-112. Various roles of the businessman and his deviation from these roles, using cultural themes as the starting point.

Cole, Arthur H. *Business Enterprise in Its Social Setting.* Cambridge, Mass., 1959, 97–134. An analysis of the various sociological factors which affect the businessman.

Hagen, Everett E. *On the Theory of Social Change: How Economic Growth Begins.* Homewood, Ill., 1962, part I. A social theory developed by an economist that helps explain the process of economic growth.

Jenks, Leland H. "Role Structure of Entrepreneurial Personality," in *Change and the Entrepreneur.* Cambridge, Mass., 1949, 108–52. A sociologist, who was interested in economic history, suggests a technique for analyzing changes in personality which occur when an individual confronts specific situations.

McClelland, David C. *The Achieving Society.* Princeton, N.J., 1961. An analysis of the motivation of businessmen experiencing economic development in societies.

Redlich, Fritz. "Economic Development, Entrepreneurship, and Psychologism: A Social Scientist's Critique of McClelland's *Achieving Society*," *Explorations in Entrepreneurial History*, 2nd ser., I (Fall 1963), 10–35. A careful critique of McClelland's book.

Scheiber, Harry N. "At the Borderland of Law and Economic History: The Contributions of Willard Hurst," *American Historical Review*, LXXV (Feb. 1970), 744–56. A critique of Hurst's work analyzing the interaction of law and socieconomic change.

Warner, R. Stephen. "The Role of Religious Ideas and the Use of Models in Max Weber's Comparative Studies of Non-Capitalist Societies," *Journal of Economic History*, XXX (March 1970), 74–99. A discussion of the application of two aspects of Weber's thought to historical studies.

Examples

Ayres, Clarence E. *The Theory of Economic Progress: A Study of the Fundamentals of Economic Development and Cultural Change.* New York, 1962.

Bruchey, Stuart. *The Roots of American Economic Growth, 1607–1861: An Essay in Social Causation.* New York, 1965, esp. chapters I, III, IV and VIII.

Cochran, Thomas C. *The Pabst Brewing Company: The History of an American Business.* New York, 1948.

———. *Railroad Leaders, 1845–1890: The Business Mind in Action.* Cambridge, Mass., 1953. *Also see* Thomas C. Cochran. "The Economics in a Business History," *Journal of Economic History*, V (Dec. 1945), 54–65.

Galambos, Louis. "Agrarian Image of the Large Corporation, 1879–1920: A Study in Social Accommodation," *Journal of Economic History*, XXVIII (Sept. 1968), 341–62.

STATISTICAL APPROACH

Brady, Dorothy. "Introduction," and Richard Easterlin, "Comment," in National Bureau of Economic Research, Conference on Research in Income and Wealth. *Output, Employment and Productivity in the United States after 1800.* Studies in Income and Wealth, XXX. New

York, 1966, 76–90. A statement of the significance of measurement and an appraisal of recent scholarship in the field.

Clapham, J. H. "Economic History as a Discipline," in Edwin R. A. Seligman (ed.), *Encyclopedia of the Social Sciences.* New York, 1931, V, 327–30. A succinct statement of the need for the economic historian to use statistics, although the author did not support the extensive adoption of economic theories or models.

Cole, Arthur H., and Ruth Crandall. "The International Scientific Committee on Price History," *Journal of Economic History*, XXIV (Sept. 1964), 381–88. A summary of activities of the group which encouraged economic historians to study the history of prices. These scholars working in the 1930s made extensive use of statistical analysis.

Heckscher, Eli. "Quantitative Measurement in Economic History," *Quarterly Journal of Economics*, LIII (Feb. 1939), 167–93. A broad definition of economic history with suggestions of many areas in which statical analysis can be used to depict economic activity through time.

Kuznets, Simon. "Introduction," in International Association for Research in Income and Wealth. *Income and Wealth of the United States, Trends and Structure.* Ed. Simon Kuznets. Income & Wealth Series II. Cambridge, Eng., 1952, 9–12. The goals of national income accounting with some of the conceptual problems associated with designing the accounts.

———. "Statistical Trends and Historical Changes," *Economic History Review*, 2nd ser., III (1951), 265–78. Cites usefulness of statistical analysis to examine long-term changes in the economies of nations.

———. "Statistics and Economic History," *Journal of Economic History*, I (May 1941), 26–41. A plea for the closer "interrelation between historical approach and statistical analysis" made at a time when few economic historians were extensively employing statistics.

Examples

Andreano, Ralph. *New Views on American Economic Development.* Cambridge, Mass., 1965, 187–225.

Bailyn, Bernard and Lotte. *Massachusetts Shipping, 1697–1714: A Statistical Study.* Cambridge, Mass., 1959.

Berry, Thomas. *Western Prices before 1861: A Study of the Cincinnati Market.* Cambridge, Mass., 1943.

INPUT-OUTPUT ANALYSIS

Christ, Carl. "A Review of Input-Output Analysis," in National Bureau of Economic Research, Conference on Research in Income and Wealth.

Input-Output Analysis: An Appraisal. Studies in Income and Wealth, XVIII. Princeton, N.J., 1955, 137–69. A summary of input-output analysis including a critical evaluation of one of the basic assumptions.

Dorfman, Robert. "The Nature and Significance of Input-Output." *Review of Economics and Statistics,* XXXVI (May 1954), 121–33. A balanced evaluation of the technique of input-output analysis.

Leontief, Wassily. "Quantitative Input-Output Relations in the Economic System of the United States," *Review of Economics and Statistics,* XVIII (August 1936), 105–25. The earliest statement of a technique to analyze the structures of economic systems. This method of analysis became an alternative to national income accounting and is still used in economic planning.

Miernyk, William H. *The Elements of Input-Output Analysis.* New York, 1965, 1–127. A nonmathematical explanation of input-output analysis.

National Bureau of Economic Research, Conference on Research in Income and Wealth. *Output, Employment and Productivity in the United States after 1800.* Studies in Income and Wealth, XXX. New York, 1966.

——. *Trends in the American Economy in the Nineteenth Century.* Studies in Income and Wealth, XXIV. Princeton, N.J., 1960.

Riley, Vera, and Robert Loring Allen. *Interindustry Economic Studies.* Baltimore, 1955. The first comprehensive bibliography on input-output analysis.

Taskier, C. E. *Input-Output Bibliography, 1955–1960.* New York, 1961. A useful bibliography published by the Statistical Office of the United Nations.

——. *Input-Output Bibliography, 1960–1963.* New York, 1964. A continuation of the preceding entry.

Example

Meyer, John R. "An Input-Output Approach to Evaluating the Influence of Exports on British Industrial Production in the Late Nineteenth Century," *Explorations in Entrepreneurial History,* VIII (Dec. 1955).

THE NEW ECONOMIC HISTORY

Conrad, Alfred H. "Econometrics and Southern History," *Explorations in Entrepreneurial History,* 2nd ser., VI (Fall 1968), 34–53, and comments by R. W. Fogel, Stuart Bruchey and Alfred D. Chandler, Jr., 54–74. A review of the literature created during the previous ten years of reevaluation.

Davis, Lance E. "And It will Never Be Literature," *Explorations in Entre-preneurial History*, 2nd ser., VI (Fall 1968), 75–92. A useful discussion of the methods of new economic historians.

Davis, L. E., J. R. T. Hughes and Stanley Reiter. "Aspects of Quantitative Research in Economic History," *Journal of Economic History*, XX (Dec. 1960), 539–47. A plea that economic historians employ modern statistical techniques and computing equipment to explore materials seldom exploited in the past in order to provide "new data and new in-terpretations of the process of economic life."

Fogel, Robert W. "The New Economic History I. Its Findings and Methods," *Economic History Review*, 2nd ser., XIX (Dec. 1966), 642–56. A concise summary of the over-all merits of the new economic history.

——. "The Reunification of Economic History with Economic Theory," *American Economic Review, Papers and Proceedings*, LV (May 1965), 92–97. Suggests the need to "sweep out the door a good deal of the old economic history."

——. "The Specification Problem in Economic History," *Journal of Eco-nomic History*, XXVII (Sept. 1967), 283–308. A call for more precise theorizing and definitions.

Hughes, J. R. T. "Fact and Theory in Economic History," *Explorations in Entrepreneurial History*, III (Winter 1966), 75–100. A leading exponent of the new economic history suggests that theory should not exclusively govern the approach of historians.

Meyer, John R., and Alfred H. Conrad. "Economic Theory, Statistical In-ference, and Economic History," *Journal of Economic History*, XVII (Dec. 1957), 524–53. Generally considered to be the first published discussion of the approach which was to be called "new" economic history. The authors suggested that contemporary economic theory or econometrics should prove an important method of analysis for his-torians.

Murphy, George G. S. "On Counterfactual Propositions," *Studies in Quantitative History and the Logic of the Social Sciences, History and Theory*, Beiheft 9, 14–38. A theoretical justification for the use of counter-factual propositions in historical studies.

Redlich, Fritz. " 'New' and Traditional Approaches to Economic History and Their Interdependence," *Journal of Economic History*, XXV (Dec. 1965), 480–95. A senior economic historian questions the newness of econometric history and stresses the interdependence between the old and the new. Redlich expands this argument in "Potentialities and Pitfalls in Economic History," *Explorations in Entrepreneurial History*, VI (Fall 1968), 93–108.

Scheiber, Harry N. "On the New Economic History—and Its Limitations: A Review Essay," *Agricultural History*, XLI (Oct. 1967), 383–95. A critical evaluation of the new economic history.

Examples

Conrad, A. H., and J. R. Meyer. "The Economics of Slavery in the Ante Bellum South," *Journal of Political Economy*, LXVI (April 1958), 95–130.

Fishlow, Albert. *American Railroads and the Transformation of the Antebellum Economy*. Cambridge, Mass., 1965.

Fogel, R. W. *Railroads and American Economic Growth: Essays in Econometric History*. Baltimore, 1964.

North, Douglass. *Growth and Welfare in the American Past: A New Economic History*. Englewood Cliffs, N.J., 1964.

Contributors

George Rogers Taylor, Emeritus Professor of Economics, Amherst College, and recently Senior Resident Scholar, Eleutherian Mills–Hagley Foundation, is the author or editor of *The Transportation Revolution* (1951), *American Economic History before 1860* (1969) and *The Early Development of the American Textile Industry* (1969) and coauthor with Irene Neu of *The American Railroad Network, 1861–1890* (1956). Professor Taylor is a former president of the American Studies Association and the Economic History Association and onetime editor of the *Journal of Economic History* and the Amherst series, *Problems in American Civilization*.

Hugh G. J. Aitken, Professor and Chairman, Department of Economics, Amherst College, and Senior Resident Scholar, Eleutherian Mills–Hagley Foundation (1969–70), is author or editor of *The Welland Canal Company: A Study in Canadian Enterprise* (1954), *Taylorism at Watertown Arsenal* (1960), *American Capital and Canadian Resources* (1961) and *Explorations in Enterprise* (1965). Professor Aitken has coauthored or coedited *The State and Economic Growth* (1959), *Canadian Economic History* (1956) and the *Canadian Commercial Revolution* (1964). He has also served as the editor of *Explorations in Entrepreneurial History* and the *Journal of Economic History*.

Alfred D. Chandler, Jr., Professor of History, Chairman, Department of History, and Director of the Center for Research in Recent American History at the Johns Hopkins University, is secretary of the Council on Research in Economic History, has served as a trustee of the Economic History Association and is on the Executive Board of the Organization of American Historians. He is the editor or author of *The Letters of Theodore Roosevelt* (4 volumes, 1952–54), *The Papers of Dwight D. Eisenhower* (5 volumes, 1970), *Henry Varnum Poor* (1956), *Strategy and Structure* (1962), *Giant Enterprise* (1964), *The Railroads* (1965). He is on the Editorial Board of the *Journal of Economic History* and *Explorations in Economic History*.

Stephen Salsbury, Associate Professor of History at the University of Delaware, is the author of *The State, the Investor and the Railroad: The Boston & Albany, 1825–1867* (1967); "The Effect of the Civil War on American Industrial Development," in Ralph Andreano (ed.), *The Economic Impact of the American Civil War* (1967); and "Statistics vs. Populist Tradition,"

Explorations in Entrepreneurial History, 2nd ser., II (Fall, 1965). In addition to other articles and reviews, he recently coauthored with Professor Alfred D. Chandler, Jr., a business biography of Pierre S. du Pont.

Thomas C. Cochran, Professor of United States History, University of Pennsylvania, has been president of the Organization of American Historians and the Economic History Association, director of the National Bureau of Economic Research and editor of the *New York University Business History Series* and the *Journal of Economic History*. He is the author of *A History of the Pabst Brewing Company* (1948), *Railroad Leaders, 1845–1890* (1953), *The American Business System* (1957), *The Puerto Rican Businessman* (1959), *A Basic History of American Business* (1959), *The Inner Revolution* (1964) and *The Great Depression and World War II* (1968). He has coauthored *The Social Sciences in Historical Studies* (1954), *History of the City of Greater New York* (1932) and *Views of American Economic Growth* (1966).

Robert E. Gallman, Professor of Economics, University of North Carolina, has served as managing editor of the *Southern Economic Journal* and is editor of the *Journal of Economic History* (1969–72). He also is a member of the Council on Research in Economic History. Among Professor Gallman's numerous articles are "Commodity Output, 1839–1899," in William N. Parker (ed.), *Trends in the American Economy in the 19th Century*, Studies in Income and Wealth (1960); "Developing the American Colonies, 1607–1783," in Douglass C. North (ed.), *Economic Forces in American History* (1964); "Gross National Product in the United States 1834–1908," in Dorothy S. Brady (ed.), *Output, Employment and Productivity in the United States after 1800*, Studies in Income and Wealth (1966); and "Self-Sufficiency in the Cotton Economy of the Antebellum South," *Agricultural History*, XLIV (Jan. 1970).

Dorothy S. Brady, Research Professor of Economics and Chairman of the Graduate Program in Economic History at the University of Pennsylvania, is the editor of *Research on the Size Distribution of Income*, Studies in Income and Wealth (1951); *Family Savings in Relation to Changes in the Level and Distribution of Income*, Studies in Income and Wealth (1952); and *Output, Employment and Productivity in the United States after 1800*, Studies in Income and Wealth (1966). She contributed an essay on "Price Deflators for Final Product Estimates" to the last volume. In addition she has written "Relative Prices in the Nineteenth Century," *Journal of Economic History*, XXIV (June 1964). Professor Brady currently serves as Book Review Editor for the *Journal of Economic History*.

Lance E. Davis, Professor of Economics, California Institute of Technology, is the author of *The Growth of Industrial Enterprise* (1964). He has coauthored with Peter Payne, *The Savings Bank of Baltimore* (1956) and with

J.R.T. Hughes and D.M. McDougall, *American Economic History: The Development of a National Economy* (1965). Among his articles are "The New England Textile Mills and the Capital Markets: A Study of Industrial Borrowing," *Journal of Economic History*, XXVI (March 1960), and "The Capital Markets and Industrial Concentration: The United States and United Kingdom Comparative Study," *Economic History Review*, 2nd ser., XIX (August 1966). Professor Davis serves on the Editorial Board of *Journal of Economic History*.

Lucius F. Ellsworth, Assistant Professor of History, University of West Florida and former Acting Co-ordinator, Hagley Graduate Program, Eleutherian Mills–Hagley Foundation, is the author of *The American Leather Industry* (1969). He coauthored with Brooke Hindle, *Technology in Early America* (1966) and coedited with Maureen A. O'Brien, *Material Culture, Historical Agencies and the Historian* (1969). Professor Ellsworth has also written "Strategy and Structure: The Du Pont Company's Sales Organization, 1870–1903," in *Papers Presented at the Annual Business History Conference* (1965), and "The Philadelphia Society for the Promotion of Agriculture and Agricultural Reform, 1785–1793," *Agricultural History*, XLII (July 1968).